I'll Be

DAMNED

If I'll **DIE** *in*

OAKLAND

I'll Be

DAMNED

If I'll DIE *in*

OAKLAND

A SORT OF TRAVEL MEMOIR

Al Martinez

Thomas Dunne Books
St. Martin's Press
New York

THOMAS DUNNE BOOKS.
An imprint of St. Martin's Press.

I'LL BE DAMNED IF I'LL DIE IN OAKLAND. Copyright © 2003 by Al Martinez.
All rights reserved. Printed in the United States of America. No part of this
book may be used or reproduced in any manner whatsoever without written
permission except in the case of brief quotations embodied in critical articles
or reviews. For information, address St. Martin's Press, 175 Fifth Avenue,
New York, N.Y. 10010.

www.stmartins.com

Library of Congress Cataloging-in-Publication Data

Martinez, Al.
    I'll be damned if I'll die in Oakland : a sort of travel memoir / by Al Martinez.—
1st ed.
        p.   cm.
    ISBN 0-312-29087-X
    1. Martinez, Al—Journeys.   2. Authors, American—20th century—Biography.
3. Journalists—United States—Biography.   4. Americans—Foreign countries.
5. Voyages and travels.   I. Title.

PS3563.A7333Z47   2003
818'.5403—dc21
[B]
                                                                    2003009041

First Edition: December 2003

10   9   8   7   6   5   4   3   2   1

To my indefatigable Cinelli,
my love, my friend, and my
traveling companion, and to
all our little travelers who
have or will someday hit
the road with us

Acknowledgments

I am indebted to my good friends Gayle Montgomery and Russell Manzatt for acting as copy readers and advisers, although I seldom take anyone's advice, and to family members who similarly offered words of wisdom and encouragement, or who just didn't say anything. Also to my agents in New York, Janet Manus, and in L.A., Jonathan Westover, I offer thanks for their standing ovations.

My editor at St. Martin's Press, Thomas Dunne, while not yet applauding, did reveal a startling patience in waiting for the manuscript. I am grateful for that, and for my line editor, Sally Kim, who tolerated with amiable equanimity my occasional bursts of angst. It's just my way.

And, assuming that all of you actually buy the book, I thank you too, even though your contribution to its creation was minimal. It's the merchandising that counts. Buy several, and don't forget Uncle Louie.

Al Martinez
Topanga, California

Contents

I'll Be
DAMNED
If I'll DIE in
OAKLAND

Prologue

This is not a where-to book or a how-to book or a how-much book. It won't advise you on what country is best to visit if you are (1) young, (2) old, (3) pregnant, or (4) on the lam. It won't tell you where to stay when you get to where you're going, how much it will cost, or what to do that is both inexpensive and fun if you are fortunate enough to do it and not get caught.

The book isn't even really about what *we* did, as a family or as a couple, where we did it, and why, except in some ways. We have been like petals in a breeze, victims to the caprice of a constant wind, blowing here and blowing there. Travel is sometimes that way, the result of a whimsical notion or a sudden urge or a shift in the wind.

But mostly travel is about time, and so is this book. Tick-tock time, year time, generations time, growth time. If you go out every day with a tape measure, you can monitor the growth of a tree. But you won't see it grow if you sit there staring at it. You've got to go away and come back and observe that what was 18 inches high is now 18.3 inches high. It matured when you weren't looking. That's the way life is.

It's the basis for a traveler's philosophy. We grow when we travel. The time spent looking at other places and other cultures is time spent not looking at ourselves. When the trip is done and we reflect on what we've seen, we realize that maybe we're a little smarter, a little more understanding, a little more compassionate. But don't plan on getting any taller, if you're about to hit the road. That's not what I mean, doofus.

Taking the kids is another way of measuring time. They *do* grow taller. And they change. You can watch the maturation process by the way they treat you and each other, and by the way they stare at the wonders around them, despite their resistance. You can't ignore the Grand Canyon even if your father is a jerk and your mother insists that you clean your room and do your homework. Kids learn as they stare that the Grand Canyon stares back. The Grand Canyon will not be denied.

So I wrote this book with a lot of things in mind. Travel, work, marriage, children, sex, growth, martinis, weather, gardens, and the family dog. They all contribute in one way or another to the great, sweeping passage of time. Children have children and the hard drinkers die. The dog runs off and Africa beckons. Fortunes rise and fall and the landscapes of our ambitions change.

I look out a window, as I write, to a view of oak trees and mountains. When we moved to this canyon paradise just a freeway away from downtown L.A. (and a Mercedes away from Malibu), the view toward the mountains was open. Now the branches of the oak trees fill half the window, obscuring much of the vista that had existed. It happened overnight, secretly, quietly, while the moon shone. That's what I mean, you see. Growth occurs when you turn away and proceeds without being noticed. It happened with the oak trees. Time passed and I wasn't even looking.

Tick, tick, tick, tick . . .

1

Mama's Boy

TO UNDERSTAND MY WILLINGNESS to travel, to spend money that ought to be used to repair the driveway or patch a leaking roof, you had to know Mary. Tough, wily, and independent as hell, she had this itchy need to be someplace else. Her children, and I was one of them, rarely got in the way of whatever trip she had in mind, whether it was to the other end of town or across state lines. Though most of her adult life was spent in near poverty (except during World War II when she was Rosie the Riveter), she more than often used what little cash she had to ride a bus somewhere, preferably to one of the Nevada gambling cities a few hours from

Oakland, where she played the nickel slots with the intensity of a brain surgeon. On one occasion she traveled to Santa Fe, New Mexico, where she was born, and another time to Texas, to visit a friend she called Dago Mary. They were the best times of her life. And she never stopped talking about them.

I learned of her travel lust during the Great Depression when I was caught stealing. It wasn't a big deal in terms of classic larceny. I was ten and as skinny as a bamboo stick and couldn't carry a lot. The ability to carry was essential to stealing back then since we couldn't afford a bicycle or even a wagon. I had to specialize in lifting small things, like ashtrays, which I sold, and bananas, which I ate. Times were hard in East Oakland. We stole to survive and to entertain ourselves. In this case it was Green Lantern comic books at Silva's Pharmacy. I was caught by Gus Silva himself, a suspected pervert, when the magazines I had hidden under my jacket slipped out and he saw them drop. I was not the best thief in town. "Gotcha, Monkey Boy!" It was a nickname I had acquired because I was in constant need of a haircut. Someone said I looked like a monkey and it stuck. I was the neighborhood monkey boy.

Gus turned me over to my mother, who was humiliated. She stole too, but that wasn't the point. It was her way that I was to do as she said, not as she did.

"You're no good!" she screamed at me. "You're a dirty crook and you'll end up in the electrical chair!" She gave me a slap atop the head. "Now we have no money for food because of you! We'll starve and our bodies will be ate by maggots!" She felt honor bound to pay Gus the thirty-cent cost of the three magazines I had been caught stealing, even though the old fool kept the magazines, and had probably stolen them in the first place. Thirty cents was big money. A quarter could buy a pound of hamburger. A nickel could buy a loaf of day-old bread.

4

My stepfather, an ex-sailor named Harry Lehman, disturbed by the yelling, walked into the room swearing and smacked me aside the head, knocking me to the floor. "Sonofabitch!" he bellowed, then walked out. I took a lot of head-hits in those days. Harry was a piece of work. Kicked out of the Navy for beating a bosun's mate half to death, he was the meanest, worst-tempered, hardest-drinking man who ever staggered the streets of Oakland. And he couldn't hold a job. My real father, whom we called Daddy Alfred, could hold a job but was also a drunk and a philanderer. My mother ran off with Harry after one Christmas when she caught Daddy Alfred, too sloshed to know where he was, urinating against the Christmas tree. He probably thought he was in a pine forest. Harry was a cook at a farmhouse over the hills in Moraga. He reeked of pork fat and whiskey. I will say in Harry's behalf that he was better drunk than sober. My mother ended up hating Daddy Alfred, who kept in touch by sending me ceramic chickens from Tijuana, where he frequently visited. Years later, we still have a cupboard full of those damned ceramic chickens.

When I was caught stealing, and this is the point of the incident, my mother hurled at me the worst condemnation that entered her mind, due to the fact that she considered me a complete failure. She screamed, "You'll never go anywhere in life! You'll never go to Santa Fe!" Then she leaned forward. "You'll never even get anywhere *close* to Santa Fe! You'll die in Oakland, monkey-boy fart!"

You have to understand the significance of this. She came from a Basque family of educators, career diplomats, and civic leaders. Streets and schools in Santa Fe are named after the Larragoites, her maiden name. They migrated from the town of Bilbao on the Atlantic coast of Spain in the 1800s when New Mexico was still a territory. They had, and continue to have, fine table manners. They never talk with their mouths full. They never pick up pork chops with their fingers or spray food when they speak. My mother some-how failed to acquire many of their cultured ways. Unable to bear her youthful hell-raising, they placed her in a Catholic convent where she was tolerated for a while, then again given the old heave-ho. Whereupon she ran off, married Daddy Alfred, a decorated World War I hero, and fled Santa Fe for Oakland.

But for all her life, Santa Fe held a mystique. She wanted to return rich, but that was not to be. She journeyed there anyhow on the Greyhound Bus to visit relatives who, as always, made the best of her different ways. It was a visit to Mecca for her, a return to her holy place of memory. She could never adjust to it as a child and really didn't understand the morality of her brothers and sisters and innumerable nieces and nephews, but she remained until her death in awe of Santa Fe.

Saying to me I would never go anywhere, surely never to Santa Fe, struck me between the eyes. The idea of living and dying in Oakland without ever having gone anywhere was, even at age ten, anathema to me, and I have been trying ever since to avoid dying on those rare occasions when I fly from L.A. to Oakland to see friends or relatives. I say to my wife, the patient Cinelli, "If you ever see me beginning to fall, turning blue with symptoms of a heart attack, place me immediately on any plane outbound from the Oakland Airport and send me anywhere else, to Kuala Lumpur, to Bangladesh, or to the Gobi Desert, but do not leave me to expire here."

Mary Larragoite Martinez Lehman, by her condemnation, had given me wings. She had created a magnesium-hot desire not only to see Santa Fe but also to visit every part of the world within reach of my budget. I made a vow that I would show her just how far I could travel. I'd be damned if I'd die in Oakland.

6

2

Monkey Boy Grows Up

AT AGE TWENTY I MARRIED a blond, bright, self-minded girl named Joanne Cinelli, who had already been to Tacoma, where she was born, and to San Diego, where she was raised in an atmosphere of refinement far different from any I had ever known. She too had been reared by a mother and stepfather, he of Portuguese blood. His father had been governor general of the Port of Macao, once owned by Portugal. He had been, in a sense, a kind of royalty among the Chinese, Antonio DeBasto Pinto Ponto Ponce de Leon Lello, taught in the European manner to scorn those of lesser status.

I was still Monkey Boy in the 1950s, but now we were called Beatniks with all our hair and our funny, airy ways. I wrote jabber-wocky poetry and sometimes slept on the sand or in the bushes at Golden Gate Park or standing up in a phone booth. San Francisco State was near Haight and Ashbury where the hippie movement was to gain prominence in the 1960s. Both Cinelli and I were students there, she a straight-A scholar universally loved and respected by everyone. I, on the other hand, spent most of my time in college arguing with student Communists at a place called the Sweet Shop that served cheap beer and open-faced roast beef sandwiches. Professors who knew us both warned Cinelli that I was a bum, but she married me anyhow after exacting a promise that I would shower daily and change underwear occasionally.

It was a year later, with her two months pregnant, that I took my first long trip, but it wasn't the one I had in mind. While I had no intention of dying in Oakland, I wasn't so sure I would have much of a choice in Korea, during that confrontation between us and the Communists that Harry Truman called a police action. Later it was elevated to the status of conflict, but never a war. I had joined the Marine Corps Reserves to earn a little extra money while attending State. Cinelli had dropped out of college to support us and was working but it wasn't enough.

My initial job as a fighting Marine was to type. I was a muster role clerk during weekly meetings of the reservists at Treasure Island, typing endless lists of names in triplicate. There could be no errors, no strikeovers, no erasures, and the list was endless. One mistake and you started over. It was hell. At one point, my mother told the Marine Corps I was a Communist. Anyone who went to college and grew long hair and read books was a Communist. A sergeant called me in and demanded to know if it was true. I should

8

have said yes. I'd have never been sent to Korea. He was a stupid man who lectured me on the American Way. "The fuckers are everywhere," he said. It was the mantra of the age, although not everyone called them fuckers. I said I wasn't a Communist. So they sent me to boot camp, into combat training, and then off to Korea.

Pusan smelled faintly like cow manure as our ship pulled up to the dock. Someone said they used human fertilizer for their crops. The smell of wood burning mingled with the stench, edging it with pine. I can smell it now. It was April 1951. Rain fell in torrents, casting the place in gray. We were marched to a mud hole of squad tents lined up in even rows, their access signified by large rocks whitewashed to stand out in the mud. It rained for three days, and then we were packed aboard a DC-3 soaking wet and flown to an airfield near the front lines. We hit the ground running and ducking and shooting. It never let up.

War is not included in most travel books. You cannot book a tour in a war. There are no decent accommodations in combat zones, not even one-star hotels or no-star hotels. But war does involve an essential form of travel that has transported young men, and more recently young women, to dark and violent places throughout history. Korea was my first big travel adventure, the only one I took without Cinelli. She waited at home, bore our first daughter, and wrote me daily. I was notified of her birth by a Marine Red Cross worker who wandered through our reserve area shouting my name. We had just come off a brutal, all-out offensive that had wiped out half our battalion. We were sick and tired and hurting.

"Marteezee!" the Red Cross guy bellowed, sloshing through the muck of our reserve area. The Marine Corps could not say Martinez. It required a sense of ethnic recognition, I guess, that was foreign to their group capabilities. The man who shouted my name

9

had an IQ only slightly higher than a duck's. I realized that I was the Marteezee he sought and said, "Yo!" which was the accepted response in the Corps.

"You married?" he demanded.

"Yo," I replied.

"Your woman had a baby."

We talked that way in those days. My woman.

"What kind?"

"Sarah or Abagail or something."

"Then we guess it was a girl baby?"

"Don't get smart-shit with me, Marteezee!"

He sloshed away, cursing. It wasn't until weeks later that I was more officially informed that it was, indeed, a girl-baby whose name was Cindy. I think we had agreed on the name because of the popularity of a song, but I'm not sure.

Someone once described war as long periods of boredom broken by moments of sheer terror. Whoever said it forgot loneliness. It's a suffocating emotion that can bring a grown man to tears, an emptiness that can't be filled, a longing that can't be satisfied when you're thousands of miles from home. But at least, I had someone to long for. Not everyone did. There was, for instance, Private X.

He was one of those flabby, nerdish guys who didn't seem to belong to any one group. He was from Iowa or one of those places that no one else in Fox Company seemed to be from. As far as anyone knew, he never received any mail or packages, which was kind of ironic because he'd been a mailman in civilian life, before the Marines called the reservists to active duty.

One summer twilight when we'd been pulled off the lines for a few weeks, we were sitting around in a reserve area drinking beer and shooting the shit when our hospital corpsman, a tall, skinny guy named Booker, who was already half drunk, walked up. He was always mixing 120-proof sick bay alcohol with powdered eggs to form a sickening eggnog as his drink of choice, and never failed to get drunk at night and sick the next day. He lived through the war, but I don't know how.

If anyone deserved to get drunk, he did. Corpsmen were right there with us on the front lines and in the attack, patching the wounded, comforting the dying, and crying their eyes out over someone they couldn't save. I remember Booker sitting alone in his foxhole, covered with someone else's blood, staring into space.

Anyhow, he came up to us that night, slightly awash, and asked if anyone wanted to get hypnotized. He'd tried it a few times before, only once successfully, turning a guy into a chicken through posthypnotic suggestion. Any diversion is welcome in war, so we all hooted and hollered for someone to volunteer. Even loaded with beer, no one wanted to end up flapping his wings and cock-a-doodle-doing like a damned fool, but then out of nowhere Private X comes wandering by.

I call him that because I haven't a clue what his name was. He was just there. Everyone started hollering for him to volunteer, and the guy was so glad to be included in something, he said okay. Booker stood up as best he could and began swinging a gold medallion he wore back and forth slowly in front of Private X and telling him to concentrate, that he's getting sleepy, sleepy, sleepy.

Damned if old X doesn't go under just about right away. Filled with self-confidence, Booker implants the suggestion that X has a candy-striped dog he loves dearly and he's holding it in his arms to protect it from being stolen from him, so precious is that dog. X, who's got a kind of dreamy look on his face, cups his arms like he's really holding a dog and begins to pet the animal.

Everyone is laughing like hell and barking and drinking beer as

X stands there looking protective and almost happy. When one of the guys gets up to try to take the dog, X, who up until then had never made an aggressive move in his life, shoves the guy so hard he ends up five feet away. X is no little guy, by the way. He's maybe six-two and weighs a couple of hundred pounds. Flabby, yes, but still big enough to cause problems.

But everyone is still having a good time when another Marine decides he's going to at least pet the dog, but X turns halfway away and won't let him. Just about then a lieutenant walks up and wants to know what the hell is going on. We tell him, and he doesn't like the idea at all. So he goes up to X and claps his hands like he's trying to snap the guy out of his trance, when X suddenly doubles up and knocks the lieutenant on his ass.

We are all suddenly silent, because no one has ever seen a private deck an officer before. The lieutenant, who is really pissed by now, gets up a little shakily and orders Booker to snap X out of it like *now!* Booker gives him a sloppy salute and heads toward X, but backs off when he sees X doubling up his fist again. Then suddenly X dashes for his tent and comes back with a loaded .45 automatic and says no one is going to touch his fucking dog.

Now it's getting serious. Everyone is telling Booker to do something before someone is killed. Booker is sobering up fast by then and has an idea. He tells X that he has some pogie-bait, a Marine term for candy, that he wants to give X's dog. Candy-striped dogs, he says, love candy. I guess it makes sense to X, who allows Booker to come close, whereupon the corpsman begins swinging his gold medallion again, and after a few moments, snaps X back into consciousness.

He's the same old nerdish guy he was, looking around like he's confused. But we aren't laughing anymore. I think suddenly we see ourselves in X, a man of such terrible loneliness that the imaginary dog represented more than we ever realized. It was a possession, a precious something that, for the few minutes he was hypnotized, filled his soul with a warmth he'd probably never known. He *belonged* at that moment, and suddenly it was over.

He smiled slightly as we dispersed to places of our own loneliness, silent and thoughtful, as the candy-striped dog trotted away over the distant hills and into the night.

I endured the indecency of front line combat for almost fifteen months. War, as I said, probably doesn't belong in a travel book, so I will spare you other details of my somewhat unpleasant stay. We came home on a troop ship called the *William Wiegle,* a two-week journey from Kobe, Japan, to San Diego. Ship arrivals weren't posted, for security reasons, so no relatives knew exactly when and where we were landing. It was night, and no one was there to greet us, not even the Marine Band, which shows up for just about everything. No music, no speeches, no relatives, no welcome home. We got on buses and were shipped to the Marine Recruit Depot to get mustered out.

When it came my turn, the guy in charge said my records showed that I'd never turned in a pillow issued during my stay in boot camp. He wasn't going to let me go home until I turned in the pillow. I guess I could have just smashed his face. I was in that kind of mood after all those months in combat. Instead, I just walked to a barracks, grabbed a pillow, and threw it at him. He knew better than to argue. Later I figured that the silence at the dock and the demand for a pillow were just the way of a surreal war no one wanted in the first place. We did what we were told, and if we lived through it, we came home to silence. So be it.

Cinelli was waiting at the San Francisco Airport when I finally got there a few days later, and so was year-old Cindy, a sweet little human who cried when I held her. She scared me. Just back from the killing fields, I was called upon to be gentle, and that was hard. I was afraid of Cindy, afraid of hurting her, of dropping her, of somehow reverting to the combat me. I could still smell Korea. I could hear screams and bombs. I cradled Cindy in my arms.

The contrast of life in my arms and death in the hills has stayed with me ever since. It's why I include war in a travel odyssey. We learn in travel, and I learned to hate the very thought of war. There are no victors, only victims. Those of us who survive repeat the horror in our nightmares long after the gunfire has ceased. I had left for the battle-fields a very young man. I had come home too sad and too old.

3

Follow the Nuns

FAST-FORWARD. It is the late 1950s. The Korean War is over but the cold war is in full swing. Dwight Eisenhower, he with the megawatt smile, is president. U.S. Senator Joseph McCarthy, a jowly drunk with immense power, is hunting down Communists, or anyone who seems to resemble a Communist. I am working at the *Oakland* by God *Tribune* on general assignment and we have another daughter, Linda, named after another song. It is an era of girl-songs, which makes the work of naming children considerably easier. Cindys and Lindas are everywhere. Our dog is Pooh, named after not a girl but a mythical bear. Winnie.

More important, I discover martinis. Like the beckoning smile of a whore in a Dutch doorway, a martini draws one to it out of primeval need. Some have compared the shape of a martini glass, that beguiling triangle, to the shape of a woman's crotch, without the stem of course. Call me old-fashioned, but I don't see the resemblance. Skip the Freudian analogy. A crotch is a crotch, a martini is a martini. It's just the lure that's the same.

The indomitable Jerry Belcher introduced me to the martini. The *Tribune* was an afternoon newspaper with six deadlines a day. We started work at 6 A.M. and most of the time were finished with the hard stuff at noon. We lunched. We drank. It was what the Trib was all about, speed and booze. Flaming typewriters, frosted glasses. At first we drank bourbon. Then Belcher, who would die from booze, discovered the martini.

"It is," he would say, his voice slurred, "like stumbling onto the wheel."

Our bar was the Hollow Leg. Three wheels a day, the third on the house.

"If you don't stop slurping down those things you're going to kill yourself!" Cinelli said to me one day. I had staggered into the house as she was visiting with the minister of a local church. We lived in the Berkeley Hills. I was wearing a clip-on bow tie in those days and came in balancing it on my nose in an effort to convince her by the facility of my equilibrium that I was sober. It had the opposite effect.

She tolerated me while the preacher was there, a painfully cheerful man who, we would learn some years later, ended up in a mental institution. That's what too goddamn much cheerfulness will do to you.

"You're drunk!" she said the minute he walked out the door, smiling broadly at something pleasant in his head.

"You're close," I said. "I am tipsy but not drunk. Drunk is when—"

"Don't tell me what drunk is. I know what drunk is. And that's where you are."

I looked out the window. Mount Tamalpais was in the center of our large picture window, hovering over Marin County in the distance. The Golden Gate Bridge was to the left, the strange, middle-dipped Richmond–San Rafael Bridge to the right. We bought the house for $11,500 on the G.I. Bill. The view was awesome.

"Your liver is going to rot, your heart is going to stop, and you're going to die," she said. "They will haul you out on your shield and dump you into the Oakland Estuary."

Cinelli is brilliant when it comes to description. The image it created was compelling. The estuary was at the time a foul-smelling body of water that fingered off of San Francisco Bay. When the tide was out, it left behind a gray muck into which one dared not venture. The muck would swallow you up like a scene from a sci-fi movie, your screams gargled, then muted as the slime embraced and filled you. I shuddered at the imagery that had been infused into our discussion of drunkenness. My boozing had gone on for several years and she was tired of it. Like father, like son. How long would it be before I pissed against the Christmas tree? "Two-Martini Martinez" she had called me at first, but when I went to three it wasn't funny anymore. She wanted me to stop. Her description of my disposal in the muck of the estuary made me think. It also triggered the memory of my mother's warning that I would die in Oakland without ever having gone noplace. Mom was talking about stealing, which I had given up. Cinelli was talking about Oakland.

"Okay," I said with a sigh that caused trees to bend along Del Monte Avenue. "I'll switch to scotch and we'll take a nice long family vacation."

So we went to Mexico.

I had just sold my first short story to a Canadian magazine called *Chatelaine*. We had five hundred dollars. It would run out before we got home three weeks later, but at that point it represented a fortune. We had also managed to save a little more from some nonfiction magazine sales, stories I had coauthored with Alex Haley. He was in the Coast Guard then, stationed in San Francisco. We were friends and together sold to *Boy's Life* and *Popular Mechanics* and a couple of other magazines I can't remember. He was years away from *Malcolm X* and *Roots*.

I loved Alex. He was more than a colleague. He was my friend. Even when he had become an American icon, he would telephone to say hello, to tell me what he was doing, and to share his wonderment at the position he had achieved. In the old days, we had drunk cheap red wine in my living room, absorbed the sparkling view, and toasted writing. The last time I saw him, he was at a head table and we were drinking expensive champagne. He looked at me over the heads of the adoring crowd, lifted his crystal glass, and winked. He was saying in his way that he was the same and we were the same, despite the high road he was now traveling. I lifted my glass in return. I never saw him again. He died a few months later of a heart attack.

Oh, Alex.

I rented a pickup truck with a Funtime Camper attached for our family vacation. Our idea was to save money by sleeping in the camper, except for big cities where we'd rent a motel room and do the town. But how could we do the town with two kids? We hired a baby-sitter to take the trip with us. She'd watch the kids while Cinelli and I played. Her name was Float. It was in that era when parents were beginning to tire of ordinary names. There were too many Sallys and Johns in the world. So her father named her Float. I never asked why.

"Will there be drinking on this trip?" her mother demanded in a tone that left no doubt about her position on boozing.

We were sitting in a living room dominated by a picture of the bleeding heart of Jesus. A crown of thorns ringed the heart. There were doilies on the couch and on the arms of two overstuffed chairs. On the opposite wall, a framed and embroidered statement proclaimed in Victorian script, God Is Love.

"Absolutely not!" I said firmly. Cinelli cast me a glance.

"No drinking," she said tightly. It was hard for her to lie.

Float was sixteen. As soon as we left the house she lit a cigarette and said, "What a lot of shit."

Cindy and Linda loved her. It was the prehippie era, and Float would be one of them someday, abandoning parents, doilies, and the bleeding heart of Jesus for the life of a flower child. Sex, drugs, and rock and roll. But at the time, despite indications of her future, she was a fine baby-sitter. Affable and open, she read and played games with our girls while parading around in a bra and red panties.

"I like her," Cinelli said, "but I'm not crazy about her red panties."

"At least she's wearing some," I said.

We drove down Mexico's Highway 1 in the Year of the Storm. We didn't know it was the Year of the Storm. It was midsummer, which was not necessarily a stormy time anywhere. Only later, while referring back to it, would Mexicans recall it as the Year of the Storm. Daddy Alfred was part Mexican. That's why he spent time hanging out in Tijuana drinking tequila and buying ceramic chickens. Before my mother kicked him out, Spanish was our family's primary language. When he left, it vanished. Harry Lehman would not tolerate spic-talk in our house. So the only Spanish I knew was what I had absorbed during high school classes, which was very little: *how much? where is? what's your name? narrow bridge,* and *beware of the cows.* "You hit a cow in Mexico and it's a life term in one of their stinkin'-ass prisons," Belcher warned. Sober, he was funny and unassuming. Drunk, he knew everything.

The storm struck as we were heading south on a flat stretch of road north of Hermosillo. Its introduction was a lightning storm beyond belief. The sky was on fire. Flashes of electricity joined to form a ring of lightning overhead. Bolts slammed into the mountains around us and into the desert we were driving through.

"Groovy," said Float. It was the word of approval that preceded *boss, bitchin', bad, crazy,* and *cool* in the lexicon of the hip. It could also be used in combinations with other words, such as *like, groovy* or *hey, y'know, groovy.* Also, *it grooves, we groove, they groove, can you dig it?*

"Turn back!" said Cinelli, who was no friend of the kind of lightning that seemed to be seeking us out.

"Turn back to where?" I shouted over the roar of thunder.

We were in the middle of the Sonoran Desert. There was nothing to turn back to.

Cinelli was in front with me. Float, Cindy, and Linda were in the camper. A window between the truck cab and the camper connected us.

"This is fun," Linda said. She was five.

"Groovy," Cindy said. She was ten and copied what Float said. We cautioned Float about that and she stopped saying *shit* in front of her . . . most of the time.

"We'll fry out here!" Cinelli shouted. The thunder was so loud it made my ears hurt. "The metal camper is like a lightning rod!"

"Don't worry," I shouted back, "we're grounded! The rubber tires will save us."

I wasn't certain I believed that. Maybe it was that we *weren't* grounded. Science wasn't one of my best subjects. "We'll be all right," I said nervously, not fully convinced. *Wham!* went the lightning. *Crash!* went the thunder.

It was raining by the time we reached Hermosillo and started looking for a place to hook up our camper. It was not a big city in those days. Not speaking Spanish made nothing easy. We used words from a Spanish-English dictionary and gestures to indicate our needs. One man sent us to a gas station. Another to a bakery. There are no words I could find to say, "We want a safe place, out of the lightning, to camp for the night. Preferably, it will have a toilet and a place to plug in for electricity."

I stopped a cop. He motioned for us to follow him. Halfway to wherever we were going he turned on his red light and siren.

"He thinks we have an emergency," I said. "When he finds out we haven't, we'll end up in a Mexican prison where brutal beatings and homosexual rape are common!" I was hanging around Belcher too much.

"Just follow him," Cinelli said. She fears very little. Only nearby lightning.

He took us to the police station, where we tipped liberally and explained to an English-speaking cop what we wanted. Three police cars led us to a campsite, Code 3. Red lights and sirens. I tipped some more. The pesos were going like tacos.

"My life," said Cinelli, observing with a shudder the lightning in the distance, "is worth a few pesos." The electrical display lasted all night. So did the rain. And in the morning, it was raining even harder.

The rain in Spain is nothing like the rain in Mexico, albeit more lyrical. The idea of rain *pouring* was born in Mexico. And this being the Year of the Storm, pouring assumed an even greater degree of violence. Rivers rose and streets flooded. Sheets of water covered even the most well-tended highways, of which there were few. Gullies became raging torrents, bridges were wiped out. Whole villages were isolated.

That degree of calamity seemed to bother no one but me. I am not a camper driver. I am not a driver of anything larger than a sedan. I felt as though I were pulling a train of boxcars loaded with *bacas*. That means "cows." Cinelli looked up Spanish words as we drove. The girls in the camper played Fish. I could hear Float shout her favorite fecal word whenever Cindy, a brilliant child, beat her at the game, which was often. My admonition to stop swearing was forgotten a day after I issued it. What the hell.

I could barely see through the storm. The windshield wipers couldn't keep up with the rain pounding against us.

"I think we ought to stop," I said.

Cinelli looked at me as though I had suggested we drive naked. "No! We've got to make Guaymas. That's our schedule."

"I can't see the road."

"Yes you can. Keep driving."

I could see her at the helm of the *Santa Maria*. "Sail on!" she'd shout. Or with Edmund Hillary on Mount Everest. "Climb on!" Or with Jacques Cousteau in the Indian Ocean. "Dive on!"

"Last night you were saying, 'Turn back,' now you want me to drive without seeing."

"You can see."

I peered through the rain-pounded windshield. "What I see now is traffic ahead of us at a stop."

"Better have a look."

I got out of the camper, bent into the wind and rain, and sought out a cop. No words were exchanged. No words were needed. The auto bridge over a wide gully had collapsed. Only a railroad bridge remained, two tracks on railroad ties set about six inches apart. The cop was directing traffic over the railroad bridge. I rushed back to tell Cinelli.

"Oh, good," she said, "then we can get across."

"Oh *good*? Death lies over that gully."

"Are we going to die?" Linda asked, picking up the terror in my voice.

"Probably," I said.

I got out of the camper again to survey the bridge. The car in front of us was loaded with nuns. They crossed themselves as the car edged onto the railroad ties, its tires straddling the rails. I got back into the camper, by this time soaked. When the nuns were halfway across, the cop waved me on.

"God help us all," I said.

"Follow those nuns!" Cinelli said.

We bumped along the railroad ties for the length of a football field. Each bump shuddered through the camper. I expected to hear a crack as the ties collapsed and then a terrible breaking as the whole bridge went and then a rush of water as we were tumbled away on the raging flood tide on our first serious family vacation.

"God wouldn't hurt nuns," Cinelli soothed. "Stay close behind them."

We made it to Guaymas, situated at the water's edge on the Gulf of California. I was a nervous wreck. We had negotiated the bridge only to face a mud-covered detour that lasted several miles. The road, as Float observed, was as slick as shit, but Guaymas seemed like paradise. It had stopped raining, and the water of the gulf was warm and so heavy with salt you could float in it.

We bobbed in the ocean and dined at a cabana on the side of a hill. When we told the waiter we were staying in a camper at the seashore, he just shook his head. Later we learned why. The heat of the night intensified as the humidity shot up. Then the mosquitoes moved in. I had not seen so many flying bugs in my life. If we closed the camper door, we'd die of overcooking. If we opened it, we'd be bitten to death.

"I can't sleep!" Cindy cried.

"I'm being eaten," Linda said.

"This is really crappy," Float said, altering her language to a more acceptable level.

A hotel in the distance gleamed like the Emerald City. We opted for it. That night shaped my attitude toward travel. Campers *no*, hotels *si*. We showered. There was air conditioning. The mosquitoes were locked out. We had only been on the road a few days but it seemed like a lifetime. In the camper, we slept in sleeping bags. In the hotel there were sheets and clean towels and a machine that made coffee right in the room. I loved that hotel. I fell asleep and dreamed that flying nuns were lifting us off a collapsing bridge and carrying us to safety, Ave Maria.

We headed for Mazatlán past towns with no names. We alternated between sleeping in the camper and in cheap motels with boarded-up windows. We ate frijoles and fish and once ordered something off the menu called "beef in its own grave."

"I'm not eating anything in its grave," Linda said.

"They mean gravy," Cinelli explained.

"It says grave, g-r-a-v-e. I want a hot dog, h-o—"

"Don't spell it!" I shouted. Other diners turned to stare.

"They don't have hot dogs in Mexico," her mother said, more calmly.

"There's a lot of shit in hot dogs," Float added.

We made Mazatlán in another rainstorm. By then, it didn't matter. The humidity would have soaked us anyhow. We rolled in late and opted for the first motel we found that had a swimming pool. Everyone jumped in, ate, and went to bed. I couldn't sleep and got up about midnight to sit by the pool. Across the patio, the bar was still open. A little brandy wouldn't hurt.

The bartender's name was José and he was a student during the day, studying law. The only other person at the bar was his friend, also named José. José One and José Two. Mexican brandy is good, and the two Josés were fine drinking companions. José One was trying to learn English. We made a deal. I would work with him on the English language, and he would furnish me with free drinks. Not since I covered a session of the California Writers Conference in downtown Oakland had I been offered so much free booze. There was a vodka fountain at the conference. It ran continuously during the cocktail hour. By the time dinner rolled around, everyone was drunk. Erskine Caldwell was the speaker, but no one listened.

José One didn't learn a lot of English from me. He already knew *cat* and *dog* and *door* and *bottle*. But we managed to communicate over drinks. José Two sang a Mexican folk tune. It made us sad. José One explained that it was about a woman who discovered her man was cheating on her. She stabbed him in the heart one night while he slept. I almost cried. Brandy makes a man melancholy.

I returned to our motel room drunk and with tears in my eyes. Cinelli hadn't even known I was gone. She awoke with a start to see me undressing.

"What in God's name have you been doing?" she demanded.

I told her about José One and José Two and the woman who had stabbed her cheating lover in the heart. My eyes brimmed over again.

"I think I can sleep now," I said.

She just shook her head.

Guadalajara. A beautiful, sophisticated city, about the size and culture of San Francisco. We got sick there. A stunningly handsome French doctor who came to our motel said it was probably from swimming in the pool in Mazatlán. Bacteria breed in warm pools. He gave us all vitamin B shots. I thought Cinelli spent an inordinate amount of time discussing bacteria with him and blinking prettily. They both blinked prettily.

"He's probably queer," I assured her.

"I don't care," Float said. "I'd do it with him anyhow."

I thought that Cindy was starting to say something but changed her mind.

Linda said, "Do what?"

No one answered.

"Do what?" she insisted.

"Kiss him," Cinelli said.

"Why?"

"Kissing makes you pregnant," Cindy said wisely.

We let it go at that.

In Guadalajara, we bought glassware. The French doctor, La Hermosa, had given us a note that introduced us to the manager at the Avalos Glass Company. He agreed to give us a discount. Cinelli went crazy. The glass was blue and beautiful. She bought tumblers and wineglasses and shot glasses and on-the-rocks glasses and pitchers and ashtrays. I couldn't stop her. I could see all our money going into glasses. We would starve in Mexico. At the end, we got the bill. It was $12 U.S. I couldn't believe it. Later, we'd have to buy a cabinet in which to keep the new glasses and a dining room set to match the glasses, which required adding onto the house. The $12 glasses eventually cost us about $10,000 U.S.

Over the Sierra Madre. The road twisted and turned. We passed trucks loaded ten feet above their guardrails. All were top-heavy, and at least three overturned on our way to Mexico City. Crowds gathered at each accident, gesturing, talking, offering advice. Buses jammed with riders sped by. Passengers clung to the back. Some were on the roof. By then, I was accustomed to the truck and its Funtime Camper. I could hum as I drove. Cinelli believes that people hum in an effort to shut out the world. She is opposed to being shut out. I don't know why I hum. My mother hummed. One of my four sisters hums. We were all trying to hum out Harry Lehman, I would guess.

Mexico City was, and still is, I suppose, at an altitude of about 7,500 feet and smoggy. With a population of 9 million, it was also busy. One drives in Mexico City at one's peril. Traffic zigs and zags, in Spanish. Horns honk. Voices rise in rage. It is Manhattan, Chicago, Boston, and L.A. combined. Rome too.

We ended up in the Hotel Polanco on the Aveneda de Edgar Poe. That was a good sign. Poe was my hero, a drunk and a poet. We dined that first night in the hotel restaurant, where I discovered tequila. It was not a discovery equal in significance to the Belcher martini, but it was important. Not the wheel but the spear. The evening began pleasantly enough until Horace Redstone walked in the dining room door. Horace Redstone and his daughter Alice.

He was six-feet-three with flaming red hair and freckles, and wore the kind of bitter smile that said he was disappointed in everyone but was trying his best to improve us all. Horace was a Baptist Bible salesman from Wichita, Kansas, full of Jesus, the Virgin Mother, and the benefits of buying the Bible in batches of a hundred with the name of your company handsomely printed without cost inside the cover. Hand 'em out to your customers, give 'em to your friends, God loves them all. Gets your name around.

Horace spotted us as the only gringos in the restaurant and asked if he could join us. I said nothing, hoping to indicate by silence that it would not be a good idea, and Cinelli smiled wanly, which was all the invitation he needed. Alice was about thirteen, I'd guess, and never said a word through the entire dinner. What their relationship was and why she was traveling with her Jesus-lovin' daddy was never made clear, but I had my suspicions. Those of us who saw the movie

Sadie Thompson know about the dark, erotic fantasies of Baptist clergymen.

Horace wanted to know first of all if we were good Christian people. I tried to discourage him by saying no, but that just added fuel to his desire to educate us on the meaning of the Bible, the intentions of God, and the money-saving value of buying the Book in batches. He ordered chicken mole, pronounced "molay" for the ethnically stupid, which is chicken covered in a rich chocolaty sauce. After he had ordered it he emphasized that nowhere in his meal should there be garlic. He was allergic to garlic. It could kill him.

As though reading my mind, the cook laced Horace's chicken with garlic. At least Horace thought he had. He took one bite of the chicken, spit it into his napkin, and shouted like a holy-rollin' preacher, "There's garlic in this goddamned chicken!" The waiter, a small man with one of those pencil-thin mustaches favored at the time, trembled with fear.

"No garlic," he said weakly, backing off.

"There's garlic!" Horace Redstone proclaimed, his voice of condemnation bellowing through the room.

He opened the napkin into which he had spat to illustrate.

"Garlic!" he said again.

The chef came out and insisted to Horace that he had not put garlic in the food, and for a moment I thought the question of garlic would end in a fistfight. A book *The Ugly American* was popular about that time, and Horace represented the prototype of the genus. During all this we tried to make the best of it by continuing to eat. Alice just stared into space, devastated by her father's tirade. There would be no Bibles sold in that restaurant. The chef finally agreed to fix Horace another dinner and allow him into the kitchen during the preparation. But as Horace was about to accept the invitation, Float stepped in. "What a shit-head," she said.

good talking to. Cindy wanted to know where the ball was, and Linda kept wondering why Float looked so sweaty.

We left Chihuahua the next morning only to get a flat tire in the middle of nowhere. The smile never left Float's face. She was in a world of her own, the joys of which we could only imagine. We were alone in the desert when the tire blew. I pulled to the side of the road, which was a mistake. The right wheels dropped into a rut. The jack wouldn't lift the camper high enough for me to change the tire. I stood there, looking over the vast emptiness of the desert. Then in the distance two Mexican men appeared. Belcher, who harbored deep suspicions of humanity in general, had warned me about banditos who preyed upon gringos broken down in remote places. "They'll cut off your balls with a rusty knife," he said with a shudder. This was the ideal setup for detesticlization.

"Get into the camper," I said in my best Marine Corps leathery gruffness. Cinelli and the others had left the camper to look around.

After a lot of whys and what-fors, they got back into the Funtime shell, and I turned, tire iron in hand, to face the banditos. It was clear as they approached that they might not be intending to rob us, kill us all, and leave our bodies to the coyotes, except maybe for Float who would probably run off with them voluntarily. They reached the camper, observed the problem, and took the tire iron from my hand while I tried to explain that I was just about to fix it, trying to sound tough and in charge.

They weren't listening. Without saying a word, they found some rocks to place under the jack so that it lifted the flat tire clear of the ground. Then they removed the tire, replaced it with a fresh one, bolted it back in, handed me the jack, and began walking away. When I tried to pay them they waved me off, probably glad that another stupid gringo was about to leave their country, a country in which they had to learn to do things on their own, without the benefits of American gadgetry.

I drove hard to El Paso and crossed the border after paying my last pesos to a Mexican cop who threatened to take me to jail because I had gone the wrong way on a one-way street. Forget that I had been waved that way by another cop. I had twenty pesos left and asked if Cop Two would give it to the judge for me, and he said sure, with the kind of look that said no judge would ever see a centavo of it.

The incident, though minor, bothered me. I wanted to remember Mexico by the guys who had fixed my tire and asked nothing in return, not by petty graft down to the lowest level of public service. But my annoyance at the crooked cop was lessened when I thought about Horace, the bombastic and demanding Bible salesman from Wichita, who probably left a trail of loathing wherever he went. There are bad guys in every culture. Eventually I found myself promising that I wouldn't stereotype Mexico by a cop on the take if they wouldn't think of all of us as clones of Horace. I made that silent deal with Mexico, and carried it with me wherever we traveled.

We drove into the good old U.S. of A., broke but grateful to be in familiar territory. In another two days we were home. I dumped the camper as soon as I could and dumped Float shortly thereafter. We never saw either of them again, which was just as well. Adios, Mexico. Hello, Oakland.

4

Don't Feed the Bikers

OUR FIRST HOUSE in the Berkeley hills was brand-new when we moved in. Before that, we'd lived in a cracker-box apartment built to accommodate the Richmond shipyard workers in Double-U Double-U Two, as Archie Bunker used to say. U.C. students and poor young journalists moved in after the fighting was over.

Our real house was on a hillside. Everything sloped, and the hard ground defied the mightiest effort to dig into it. But we dug anyhow. I learned to lay bricks and concrete blocks, and Cinelli bent to the task of creating a garden. How she managed to make anything grow in the hard soil of Arlington Mountain ranks along with the mysteries of the pyramids. We wonder how the Egyptians did it. Now they wonder how Cinelli broke through the clods and the adobe to fashion a garden on the corner that everyone who passed admired.

It changed with the seasons, blooming in the sun and dying in the cold winter winds that swept in off the bay. My walls surrounded it, built over months, brick by brick, painstakingly joined with steel and concrete to last forever. They're still there. Not a crack in them. And the garden still grows, though the years have passed. Gardens defy time if they're done right. They swing with the years, dancing to the pulse of seasons that alter them. That's time, you see.

Cinelli sees a new house as a blank canvas. I see it as a money pit, a hole to toss hundreds if not thousands of dollars into, a place from which it never reemerges. Granted, it improved the house on Del Monte Avenue, but it also left us broke.

"I'm sorry this cuts into your martini money," Cinelli said, "but maybe you can make do with an occasional beer."

To suggest that an Oakland newspaper reporter drink beer was to suggest that the Queen of England take a bus to Buckingham Palace. They are both simply unthinkable. But houses are important to Cinelli. They were then, they are now. And a garden draws her to its breast like a secret lover. She romances the roses and causes perennials to bloom to her smile. Money spent on house and garden is money offered to gods beyond my knowledge.

But still, the need to travel also beckons. So where do you go when there's no money to go elsewhere? One goes, shudder, camping.

My idea of camping has altered over the years from sleeping in a tent to bedding down in a hotel rated at less than three stars. Roughing it has come to mean dinner without wine. But in the 1960s, earning about $150 a week at the *Oakland Tribune*, camping involved pitching a tent in state and national parks and sometimes in primitive U.S. Forest Service camps where there were no showers and the outhouses were a half mile away through woods filled with wild bears.

But I discovered a kind of peace in the outdoors that one doesn't always find in the bustling cities of the world. My memory of camping is softened by a fragrance of pine in the warm air and by a sunset breeze whispering through the tall trees. It's just the damned bears that drove me crazy.

I think of bears the way I thought of Chinese soldiers during the Korean War, capable but evil. Bears are the enemy. Unlike human combat, however, one is forced to face them unarmed. Bears rip open metal food containers. They scratch at cars, ransack luggage, and lumber about through human-occupied areas half the night. Warning signs do not bring comfort to families who camp. Stories abound of bears attacking campers.

"We're going to die on this stupid family trip!" Cindy shouted. She was thirteen and evolving slowly into a gorilla. Family trips irked her. She wanted to do her own thing. That was the motto of the decade. What her own thing might be was not something I felt I wanted to discuss with her. It was the era of not trusting anyone over thirty.

"Bears don't kill people," Linda said. She loved animals. It was inconceivable to her that any animal would do her harm.

"They'll rip your freaking head off!" Cindy screamed, edging away from a snorting outside the tent.

"What did you say?" I demanded.

"I SAID THEY'LL RIP YOUR . . ." Pause. "I didn't say that."

"You didn't say what?"

"I didn't say what you thought I said."

"They won't rip your freaking head off," Linda said.

Women had come a long way in the 1960s. They had become

more aggressive in their sexual pursuits, more open in their language. Fuck War was inscribed on a banner strung across 13th Street near the Tribune Tower by a group out of Berkeley that called itself the Bitch Brigade for Peace. Women campaigned for their right to multiple orgasms as though it were guaranteed in the U.S. Constitution. They burned their bras and talked about the chauvinistic male pig.

"Don't ever say that again," Cinelli admonished our girls.

We both knew it was a futile gesture. Haight-Ashbury was in, parental guidance out. Mix teenage into a pot that includes cultural revolution and what emerges is a heady brew. The young drink it up. Lenny Bruce was doing an act that talked about the beauty of the F-word. It defined an act of love, he said. It meant creation. "F-you, Mom. F-you, Dad." Then they arrested him and threw him in the freaking slammer.

Contrary to a Greyhound Bus slogan at the time, getting there was never half the fun on a long drive to a campsite in the mountains. Not for us anyhow. Linda was thirsty and had to go to the bathroom the minute we left the driveway.

"We're not stopping!" I shouted. I shouted more as a father with young children than I do now. Kids do that to you. That was in direct opposition to a growing misconception that children should be treated as small adults. You sat down with them and reasoned. You explained. You used logic. I tried all that and it didn't work, so I shouted.

"I have to go to the bathroom bad!"

"Badly," Cinelli corrected.

"NO YOU DON'T!" I shouted.

"I do!"

"YOU DON'T!"

36

Once I am in a car and rolling, I am locked in. My go button is pushed. As a shark must forever swim forward to remain alive, I must drive forward to remain sane and happy on a trip.

"Okay, I'll just wee-wee all over the car then!"

The Car. It was my first new car, a Chevy. It didn't have a scratch on it. No one had ever urinated in it before. To have thus defiled it would have been an atrocity equal to the sacking of Carthage or the rape of the Sabine women.

"You'd better stop," Cinelli said. "She may have a defective bladder. We'll have a surgeon open her up and take a look. Pull off at the next doctor sign."

Silence from the backseat.

"That's funny," Linda said, "I don't have to go anymore."

She was bored. And when children are bored, it is incumbent upon parents to amuse them. One method was to engage in car fun. Into that era with its maddening ritualistic tendencies came I Spy with My Little Eye, a game invented by psychotics to be played in moving vehicles.

It works this way: The person whose turn it is says, "I spy with my little eye something that begins with . . ." and then you say a letter from the alphabet. For example, it's Cindy's turn. She sees a tree. So her little eye spies something that begins with a *T*.

"It's a truck," Linda says.

"No it isn't, stupid."

"She called me stupid!"

"Well, she *is* stupid."

"Don't call your sister stupid." It's a phrase said by parents in unison. We have said it many times before.

Cindy throws up her arms in disgust. In so doing, her hand brushes Linda.

"She hit me!"

"I did not!"

"I just did this." She repeats the gesture, again brushing Linda's arm.

"She hit me again!"

"I just touched you, stupid! *This* is a hit!"

She demonstrates by giving Linda a whack. Linda whacks back. Soon they are whacking with vigor.

"Good God, separate them!" I shout.

"Okay," Cinelli says pleasantly, "stop the car. I'll put one in the trunk and drape the other one over the hood."

I stop the car. "You heard your mother," I say. "Into the trunk, Cindy."

Cinelli opens the trunk.

"You, Linda, climb up on the hood."

They look at us, not quite sure what to make of the whole thing. Then Linda says, "How come she gets the trunk and I have to be on the hood?"

We are at a loss for words when Cindy, in an uncommon burst of generosity, says, "She can have the trunk if she wants. I'll take the hood."

Cinelli shakes her head and begins to laugh. Then I laugh. Cindy, realizing the absurdity of it all, joins in. Linda, still puzzled, wants to know, as we climb back into the car, who gets the hood? We play I Spy all the way to the mountains.

One camping trip involved several stops up through California and into Oregon and Washington State. The first stop was about a half mile from a beer bar that was a biker's heaven. It was (shudder) the era of the Hell's Angels. The Vietnam War was in full swing, anti-war rioters were raising hell in the streets, and the Angels had turned suddenly patriotic. Because I was covering the riots for the

Trib, Sonny Barger, the ultimate Oakland Angel, wrote me a letter, meant to be published as is, in which he offered to serve as a guerrilla in the war. Well, actually, *gorilla* was the way he spelled it. And a gorilla he could have been. The United States Government gratefully and very politely declined the offer.

I thought I saw Barger in the bushes when we camped about a mile from the beer bar/pool hall in the Sierra Nevadas. It was near a lake, and on a quiet night one could hear the croaking of bull frogs and the howls of bull bikers floating on the summer air.

"They'll come for us," I said to Cinelli. "I can feel it in my bones."

"I don't think it's you they'll have in mind," she said.

"Your karma is all wrong," Cindy said. "You're giving out negative vibes."

"Oh, well," I said, "in that case, let's all hum together and everything will be just fine. There is no violence in the alpha state."

"Parents," Cindy said, making a sound of disgust and stomping off. I thought I heard her say, "To hell with you all," but I wasn't sure.

It was at twilight when I saw Sonny Barger. The men's bathroom was about a hundred feet away. I was walking toward it through a pine forest when I heard a noise and then spotted a bulk in the shadows coming toward me. It was Sonny, I knew it. He'd been on my mind all the time we were at that damned camp because of the proximity of the biker's bar. He was there, drooling and growling in the darkness, waiting for the opportunity to wreak his lust on my young and voluptuous wife.

I had just read a short story in one of the men's magazines I was beginning to write for. I think it was *Cavalier* or *Argosy*. Or maybe just *Man*. A group of bikers had followed a young couple they'd spotted at a gas station. They cut them off at an isolated road. The wife was sexually frustrated due to an uninterested husband. She was horny, he wasn't. She was a looker in an angora sweater. The lead biker carried her off into the bushes and had his way with her, as we used to say. Rape wasn't invented until years later. The husband, a frightened little man, did nothing. Afterward, the bikers roared off and the wife screamed at her Milquetoast guy that she'd loved every minute of it.

Perhaps I could make a deal with Sonny. My two daughters when they're of age if he leaves my wife alone. Okay, my two daughters and my car. My two daughters, my car, and fifty dollars. My two daughters, my car, fifty dollars, and rights to my wife when she reaches fifty.

The shadow in the forest paused. Then it fell on all fours. One thing I always admired about Sonny Barger. He always walked upright. Then if it wasn't Sonny Barger . . .

"It's a bear," Cinelli said matter-of-factly. She had come up behind me, wondering where I was.

"Don't move," I whispered, picking up a fallen branch.

"You're going to fight a bear with a twig?"

"Not so loud," I whispered again.

"Right," she whispered back, "he might hear you."

I whacked the branch into the palm of my hand. It broke in two. Cinelli rolled her eyes skyward. I looked for another weapon and came up with a rock. The bear, meanwhile, had moseyed off. When I looked up, he was gone.

"Can we talk normally now?" Cinelli whispered.

Bears were everywhere, disgusting their breed by begging at cars and eating garbage. Food near a tent was an invitation to the beasts to join you for dinner. Refuse them and they eat you. Because they are related to pigs, bears snort. Nothing that snorts is a friend of mine. We had a reporter at the *Tribune* who snorted. Everyone hated him for it, even though he consistently won Press Club Awards. How could a guy who snorted win anything? In addition, he wrote about boring things like transportation. He was a boring snorter.

The bears were so bad one night, we abandoned the campsite and stayed in a cabin. The next morning we went back for our tents and left. Moments like that help define travel by offering up the unexpected. You have to adjust to the conditions that prevail. We adjusted by leaving bear country and heading into mountain lion country.

One may look upon bears as bumbling garbage-eaters, but mountain lions are something else. While they may consume, say, a dead and rotting deer now and again, they are mostly sleek and efficient predators. They would rather dine on live prey. There were no signs to warn us as we hiked up Washington's Mount Rainier that there were any of the cats around. There were. I was carrying Linda on my shoulders up a slight incline because she was tired and thirsty and I don't play I Spy on the trail. We had rounded a kind of bend in the trail when there he stood (or maybe there she stood) about twenty feet away. I spied with my little eye something that began with mountain lion. I froze. He had stepped out of a clump of underbrush, his tail twitching, and was staring at me with the kind of stark intensity that said he was wondering if I, or any one of us, was good to eat. Think of yourself at an unknown restaurant staring down at a piece of unrecognizable meat and wondering the same thing. Now think of yourself as the meat.

Realizing I had stopped, Cinelli, who was leading the way, turned back to see if I was goofing off. Later, she would recall the stricken look on my face. She had heard that veterans of war often flash back to combat situations and occasionally go on rampages in the mistaken belief that they are still fighting enemy soldiers. But before she could shout, "The war's over, stack arms!" she followed my gaze to the mountain lion.

"Hmmm," she said, observing the creature, its shoulder muscles rippling, its eyes as cold as snow.

I have never known Cinelli to panic, although she approached it that time in Mexico when lightning danced in the skies. "Hmmm" was about as close to a scream of terror that she ever got.

I'm not sure if it was the threatening tone of the *hmmm* or simply the animal's decision that there was nothing appetizing here, but he turned with a swish of his tail and disappeared back into the thicket. Up to that time, neither Cindy nor Linda had said a word. Then Linda said, "That was a big cat."

Cindy, barely able to speak, said, "It was a lion, stupid."

Why include a chapter on camping with kids in a book of travel? Because every journey adds to the sense of vastness in our souls, whether it's over a mountain or halfway around the world. The same spirit that pushes explorers across oceans and into space moves us all to a lesser extent. And through the eyes of children we discover what we've already seen but never absorbed. We learn from them even as they learn from us.

Years later our kids still talk about the fun in the calamity of family vacations and the peace of the forest on sweet summer nights. And I still think about them establishing their individual personas, asserting their right to be heard in a world where only the most determined voices are acknowledged. I can still see the wonder in their eyes by the campfires of my memory, and I know just how much, in those gentle moments, that they edged toward adulthood, better for their memories.

THE 1960S EXPLODED OUT OF HISTORY. *Not the decade, the era.* *Like time and growth, they had begun to build unnoticed in the coffee-houses of San Francisco and on the campus at Berkeley. They were fueled by the headlines of war and racism and by the satire that sizzled like burning wicks into the explosive mixture. The war in Vietnam was growing and so was a movement among blacks for their share of the American pie. Add to that the shouts of women rising above the crescendo demanding equal treatment and you have a moment in history louder than trumpets and more deafening than drums. I loved it.*

I was a left-wing, rabble-rousing columnist for the Oakland Tribune, *a job so weird and incongruous that it probably never should have happened. I was, as one reader suggested, the lipstick on a gray lady. The publisher of that old gray lady was also a gray personage, one William Fife Knowland, a right-wing Republican and former U.S. senator, who saw any movement for peace and equality as a Communist plot. There was bound to be trouble between us.*

I campaigned for all the causes that were popular among dirty Berkeley punk liberals, folksingers, transcendental meditationists, Hare

Krishnas, out-of-body levitationists, and Zen prayer leaders. Things like peace, love, equality, and Alice B. Toklas cookies. Knowland stood in awesome opposition, like a leviathan at the gates of hell. We soon defined our positions on the paper. My job was to write the column, his job to kill it. "Do it my way," he warned, "or not at all." That's how we ended up in L.A.

We had a son then. I wanted to name him Pluto after the Disney character popular at the time, but Cinelli would have none of it. We named him Allen. He was born on the birthday of Kazimierz Pulaski, a Polish patriot. We could have named him Kazimierz. The girls called him Marty. Cindy, Linda, and Marty. Right out of Americana.

Marty was five when my job fell apart. It was in the fall of 1971. I walked away with a nice pocket full of change and a job offer at the L.A. Times. *But there was pain involved too. The transition was major, leaving behind a home we loved in an area where I had grown up. Los Angeles was a colorless splotch on the map of Southern California, a place we made fun of, the butt of jokes.*

We were living in the suburbs then at the foot of Mount Diablo, so named because the face of the devil appeared on its surface when the flat white light of the late afternoon threw shadows over the south face. We had an acre of land, a swimming pool, a garden, a redwood deck I had carpentered with my bare hands, and a room I had helped build. Rain fell on this place and fog crept in through gaps in the hills that faced toward the bay. There was weather here. The leaves of silver-dollar trees shimmered in the winds that whistled down off Diablo. There was no weather in L.A., only the strange red irresistible sun glaring through the smog.

Time leaves memories in its wake. They lie where they were born and grow dimmer with distance as one moves away. I left many in the Bay Area. Memories in San Francisco and memories in Oakland. Our children were born here. They grew here, their lives expanded by small trips, their character molded by their surroundings. I was aware of the monumental nature of the move, the personal trauma I was undergoing, and the vacancy I was stepping into. I was more conscious of time than I had ever been. It was a thunderclap that dominated my senses, leaving me more than a little disoriented.

"Upward and onward," Cinelli said holding my hand, perceiving my pain. "To hell with Oakland. Let's take a trip."

5

Heaven, Hell, and L.A.

IT WAS EITHER L.A. OR D.C. The *Washington Post* had also offered me work, but I'd rather live in hell than anywhere near Washington. So we chose hell. Southern California's only plus was the *L.A. Times,* a writer's paradise in those days, big and rich and prestigious under Otis Chandler. I looked back at the Bay Area with some longing and then turned away. We took a trip.

"Think of it as a transition," Cinelli said. "We'll rent a camper and take the kids out of school and bring the dog with us!"

"Like hell we will," I said.

Cindy was in college and Linda in high school. Marty was about to start first grade. We had blinked, and they had grown. The dog was a pathetic and possibly psychotic no-breed animal named

Barney, with beady, close-set eyes and an arrogant attitude. He could have been the love child of an unholy union between Richard Nixon and Bebe Rebozo.

"I like the part about staying out of school," Linda said.

I said, "We are not renting a camper again, we are not taking the stupid dog, and we are not . . . What was the rest of it?"

"Staying out of school," Cindy said helpfully.

"Not that either."

"We'll vote on it," Cinelli said.

"This is not a democracy."

"It's more like a theocracy," Cindy said. Being in college, she naturally knew everything and was not averse to showing it.

"That's really dumb saying that," Linda said. She was in high school and *almost* knew everything.

"We're just not going to do it," I said. "I'll never, I mean *never*, take any kind of a trip in a camper again, I will not take the dog, and it would be unconscionable to keep the kids out of school."

Cinelli smiled.

Two weeks later I was at the wheel of a pickup with a camper attachment heading north out of Oakland. Things happen fast with Cinelli. If she says, in her disarming fashion, "It would be fun to visit East Timor," you can bet your last Timorian nickel we'll be there before the season sets. She has sought the path least taken for most of her life, but she knows that in order for me to accompany her she has to promise a certain degree of comfort and safety. Her appeal this time was that our girls were nearing the marrying stage and we ought to take a full-family vacation before they were up and gone.

"This might be our last family vacation," she said, addressing whatever limited sense of sentimentality I possessed. Then she said,

"Have a nice cool martini, dear, and think about it," knowing how, like the dreaded Harry Lehman, I soften when my antagonisms are damped by a little something, as Pooh might say. His reference was to honey and not necessarily to a martini, although I have my suspicions.

Once more we had rented a camper attached to a pickup. A window opened between the camper and the cab so that we could keep in constant touch, just like in Mexico so many years before. The idea was to cross the United States via a northern route, ending up on the East Coast, and returning via a southern route, concluding in the city of our future, L.A. We departed in late summer with everyone singing campfire songs and the dog barking. Barney barked for the thinnest of reasons, and often for no reason at all. He barked at stars and cowered when a strong wind blew and barked into it. He barked at the dishwashing machine and at the hum the refrigerator makes, standing a good distance away in the event that the refrigerator, fed up with his incessant yammering, would suddenly lumber toward him and eat him alive, yowling and barking.

It was raining when we reached Seattle, which is not unusual for the Northwest. It was not, however, the kind of drenching, pouring, killing rain we had encountered in Mexico, the rain to end all rains. I could tolerate a little sprinkle on the fiberglass roof of our Aljo camper as we rolled along with "Someone's in the Kitchen with Diiiinah." Under normal conditions, I can't stand the song, and I suspect Cinelli isn't crazy about it either, but she would rather hear me singing than humming, especially when I am listening to one tune on the radio and humming another. While that takes a kind of schizophrenic talent, it is nothing compared to that of a man I knew on the college newspaper at San Francisco State who could hum and type stories in the rhythm of the tune he was humming. The paper was housed in a metal quonset hut left over from the Second World War, and sound resonated. On some days the typerhummer's rhythms would fill the room, and eventually we'd all be typing in that rhythm like a kind of clickety-clacking Mormon Tabernacle Choir. Weird college days.

After a while singing got almost as tiresome as I Spy, so we switched to license-plating. That involved looking for plates from different states. At one point, Linda remarked that there were sure a lot of Wyoming plates. "That's because we're in Wyoming," Cindy said. She almost added "stupid," but didn't, which shows we were gaining ground in their development. But license-plating became such an intense contest we dropped it after a while. I suggested an activity at which I prevail: lesbian-spotting.

"You look for certain features," I explained, "such as a manly walk, the tendency to spit and adjust your testi . . ."

I could tell by her expression that Cinelli didn't want to spot lesbians. My words faded. It was back to Dinah in that goddamned kitchen.

"What's a lebsian?" Marty said.

Barney was the unknown factor in our three-month trip. I could accept as part of my fatherly responsibility that someone in the family would often be thirsty, carsick, or have to go to the bathroom. Boredom was no longer a factor, nor, oddly, were too many family arguments. The girls doted on Marty, who seemed to accept whatever came along. But the dog was something else. Having to stop to walk him or to watch the door so that he wouldn't escape or to sneak him into a trailer court that didn't allow pets introduced an element into the trip that was, to say the least, unusual. This was not a dog that traveled well, not at all like Steinbeck's Charley. Someone always had to be in charge of Barney lest he suddenly break free . . . and breaking free seemed his only goal in life. That and his endless barking, which made sneaking him into no-dogs-allowed places difficult. A motel clerk, hearing Barney's muffled bark from the camper (we sometimes held his snout shut to silence him) remarked that it sounded like one of our kids had the whooping cough. We smiled and said yes that was it, while Barney struggled to be heard.

Up through Oregon into Washington and a discovery: wind is to a camper what sharks are to abalone divers. It comes from nowhere, bashing into the broad side of a so-called recreational vehicle the way a great white smashes into the side of a scuba diver. We discovered this crossing over the Cascades from Washington into Idaho and down into Montana. I remember it clearly. We were singing a college drinking song I had introduced into the mix when *whammo!*, a shudder went through the camper and the music stopped. We rocked and rolled over the mountains for the rest of the day, with Marty taking over Linda's childhood job and wanting to know if we were going to die. A gas station attendant said later that only a fool would drive a camper east to west over that five-thousand-foot pass in a seventy-mile-an-hour wind blowing from north to south. I said, "That's us!" as brightly as I could. He just shook his head.

Then the snow came and the temperature dropped to twenty-four degrees. The roads narrowed and twisted. Silence prevailed. Even Barney didn't bark. We stopped at every small town we encountered, the way Bedouins exist from oasis to oasis. The towns had names like Opportunity, Crackerville, and Smelterville. The stores had toilets, but you couldn't use them unless you bought something. Cheese puffs were cheap and plentiful, so we bought cheese puffs at every stop.

"I'm sick of cheese puffs," Cindy said. "I'd rather explode from lack of a toilet than eat another cheese puff."

"Me too," Linda said.

They had a secret handshake they performed when in agreement, which was becoming more often. My girls were growing up. Only occasionally did words like *dumb* and *stupid* creep back into their vocabulary. Accidentally touching each other was no longer a major violation of personal space. I do not mean to imply a total lack of disagreement. A major bone of contention involved whose turn it was to sit in the front seat next to me. The front seat was a privileged place. I would allow them to work it out, removing myself as much as possible from the fray while they created a specific mileage/time schedule as complicated as a rocket launch. Mostly it was Cinelli sitting next to me, charting our way across the mountains and the plains. Only once did Barney occupy the coveted right-hand seat, barking all the way.

Yellowstone National Park was murder. Forget that it was in the middle of a snowstorm and roads were closing everywhere. Everyone wanted to see Old Faithful, a spout of hot water, that shoots periodically into the air. I had no such need to view hot water, and even the park ranger at the gate wondered why we were there in such lousy weather. He failed to understand the dynamics of family. An idea emerges, builds, and assumes a life of its own. We were Hannibal crossing the Alps, Attila conquering Rome, Admiral Peary sledding to the North Pole. The road was as slick as a politician's promise and the snow blinding. I drove as close to the geysers as allowable and everyone got out.

I had not encountered such cold since I was in Korea. Only the dog was not out in it, rather peering from a window barking wildly and looking as though he wanted nothing more in the world than to run through the snow.

"Please, can't we let him out?" Linda the animal lover begged.

"He'd run off and be a dogsicle in this cold," Cinelli said.

"I'll leash him," Linda promised.

"There is no leash made that will hold Barney," she said. "He will drag you across the snow and into the geysers."

"The dog is as dumb as a chair," I said.

"Inanimate objects do not have brains," Professor Cindy interjected, "although plants are said to be able to respond to music."

The wind picked up, icing through us like needles. More snow fell. "For sure we're going to die out here," I said. I felt the way members of the Donner Party must have felt. Soon we would have to decide which of us to eat. Barney would go first.

"Have we seen enough hot water yet?" I demanded, shivering. So close to hot water, so near to freezing.

We agreed that it was time to leave. But couldn't. These were the days before every vehicle on the road had four-wheel drive. No SUVs then to plow through crap and corruption loaded with young studs and beautiful willing women on their way to beer and sex and other forms of high adventure. I love those TV ads. The SUVs are always red, the women always hot. The male actors in those commercials are probably gay, which makes it even more enticing. A real guy like me comes along and the women go crazy from the sexual heat, screaming for it like animals, hoo-boy.

Our camper wouldn't go because it was stuck in the snow and the slush. The motor roared and the tires spun and the dog barked, but the vehicle didn't move. "We're doomed," Cindy offered helpfully. Hers was a sense of humor dangerously paralleling my own. "It's a curse," Cinelli remarked. "She will go through life challenging and ridiculing and growling."

A dented and paint-scratched pickup rolled into view out of nowhere, no doubt summoned by the roar of my engine, the way the call of a bull moose lures a potential mate. Singles bars have similar signals. Two men got out of the pickup, one holding a bottle of whiskey. It was the Mexican desert all over again, with snow. But this time, Jack Daniel had become a factor. There was not a ranger in sight, only me and two drunken drifters.

"You look like you need a drink," the one with the bottle said, laughing and handing it to me. His name was Ben, the other one Larry. I could see the headlines: *Ben and Larry Killers Strike Again! See Page 24 for details.*

"I could stand a swallow," I said. I am not averse to sharing a drink with a friend, even if it is whiskey, which I normally do not drink. But Ben was not a friend. They were bearded and unkempt and smelled faintly of beer and urine. Some bars in Oakland smelled that way. Harry Lehman loved them, especially one downtown called Crabby Joe's that played country music and offered free hard-boiled eggs.

"I'll get some boards," Larry said, spitting into the snow. "Tell your old lady it'll be okay." He blew a kiss toward Cinelli, whom I had ordered back into the camper along with the kids. They stared through the window at us. Poor Daddy, out there with dirty and ragged and smelly thugs. Poor me.

But you know what? It *was* Mexico all over again. Good guys in bad clothes ennobling the human spirit by doing a little something for someone else and asking nothing in return. They put boards under the tires, and after a few tries I got the camper out onto the main road. I had another drink with my new friends, Ben and Larry, offered them enough money for another bottle, which they refused.

"You never know," I said as they drove away.

"If this keeps up," Cinelli said, "you might learn to love the human race even before a second martini."

"Maybe."

We headed out. Well, almost out. Cinelli wanted to try a road that wound down into the canyon. I started to go that way and then was taken with an epiphany. God talked to me and said, "To hell with it, don't go." Cinelli shrugged. "I'm not taking on God," she said. We found the only motel in the area that was open, got their last room, bought cheese puffs and buffalo jerky at a store that offered little else, and went to sleep warm and grateful to be alive, singing "Oh Susanna." Don't you cry for me.

Billings, Rapid City, Sioux Falls, Sioux City, Cedar Rapids. We rolled eastward through the autumn. Years later I would reflect on the trip through the fall as a metaphor for the changing seasons of our lives. The journey was elemental. Cindy and Linda were growing more serious about themselves, girls becoming women. Marty was emerging from infancy to boyhood. And soon a new life would open up for us in L.A. The changing colors of autumn matched the changing nature of our lives. It was too bad we had to live it in a camper.

Only infrequently did we find campsites to my standards. They were usually located at recreational vehicle stops called KOA for Campgrounds of America. Or Kampgrounds, I guess. They had hookups for electricity and water and well-stocked stores and clean bathrooms and were generally not populated by someone wanted for armed robbery in Wyoming. Mostly they were retired people trying to get away from their children and their past. They drank and played bridge and were prone to saying, "Howdy, neighbor." But I guess they had to say something.

Not all the places where we stayed were so clean and amiable. I remember one somewhere near Grand Rapids. Trailer Trash Inn. There were no showers and the toilets closed at nine. "Why?" I asked the strange and angry lady in her rundown shack of an office. Why did the toilets close at all? She replied, "You questioning me, mister?" I had the odd feeling that if I were questioning her, mister, she would reach under the counter, produce the kind of long-barreled .44 revolver Wyatt Earp used to pack, and shoot me dead on the spot. So I said, "Oh, no, I just wondered. That's a good idea, closing at nine, I think I'll do that at home."

"You're going to close our toilet at nine?" Cinelli said, giggling, as we walked away.

"I'd close it at seven if she said to."

This is where the guy wanted for armed robbery in Wyoming stayed. In fact, it may have been one of those secret hideouts for felons of all kinds who got together occasionally for a sort of criminal reunion, exchanging stories of their last rape or murder or arson. They partied all night and for reasons known only to God gunned their engines off and on. Cinelli suggested I go out and ask them politely to keep the noise down, which would have been like asking the Arabs to lay off the Jews. We bore the calamity as best we could and left at dawn.

We had to see Niagara Falls. This was the place of honeymoons, of crazy people riding the cascade in barrels and dying in foam, of tightrope walkers daring the distance over the falls and falling and dying in the foam next to the people in the barrels. And it was where Barney broke for freedom. I'm not sure how it happened, but suddenly there he was, out of the camper and racing toward a bridge that crossed over into Canada. Barney hates confinement. At home, we built him a fenced-in yard and he figured out how to climb over the fence. We raised the height of the fence and he dug under it. We placed stakes down to three feet and he still managed to find weak places into which he would cram his body and wiggle until he was out on the street, running. Keep him in the house and he'd pound his head against the door until someone let him out into the yard, where he roamed the fence like a prisoner of war, seeking a way to escape.

I stayed with Marty while Cinelli and the girls went after him. I was personally content to let him dash across the border, request asylum, and spend the rest of his days in Quebec City. Not a bad life. Learn a little French, adapt to escargot, wash 'em down with a nice pinot noir. "Let him go," I shouted after the running females. "He'll be better off among the Canadians." But they wouldn't give up, and finally caught Barney when he stopped to relieve himself. If it hadn't been for nature, he'd have been on the bridge.

"I could kill him," Cinelli said, panting.

"Why not?" I said. "Just a little nudge as we stand at the rail over the falls and . . ." I made a gesture of one going down into the foamy water at the bottom of the falls, next to the tightrope walkers and the barrel-riders.

"Don't kill Barney," Marty said seriously.

"He won't," Linda assured him. "He's just goofy."

Off to New York City.

Seeing Manhattan for the first time is like falling asleep in your own bed and waking up naked in the middle of a circus. Clowns, elephants, jugglers, pickpockets, hookers, circling yellow taxis, three rings all going at once. I tried driving the camper through Manhattan on garbage pickup day, each narrow side street blocked by over-sized garbage trucks, intersections impossible to navigate, streets like rivers of taxi-yellow blood. I couldn't have felt more vulnerable if I *were* naked. Driving that thing around in the valley of skyscrapers made me feel like we were the Joad family coming to town looking for work pickin' fruit.

I parked the camper in North Bergen, New Jersey. I'd have gladly pushed it into the Hudson River, but didn't. We left Barney with the couple who owned the trailer park. They'd watch him for an extra five dollars. The woman had no teeth. The man was blind in one eye and wore a black patch over it.

"I don't like them," Linda said. "They might kill Barney."

"Yes," I said, "they might. Hurry children, we've got to catch a bus."

New York. So wild and yet so enchanting. We took subways and rode buses. Taxi drivers wouldn't take five people in one cab, only four.

"We're just going to have to leave someone," I said to Cinelli. It was raining in New York, as it does whenever we travel, and taxis could become an essential means of transportation. "We have two girls and only one boy, so how about dropping one of the females? We can always do with just one."

"I've got a better idea. I don't intend getting pregnant again, I can drive and I can work, so why not just leave *you*? Good idea?"

"I'll drink to that," Cindy said.

"You'll drink to nothing," her mother said. "You want to turn out like your father?" Then she turned to me. "Just kidding, dear."

When we weren't touring, we were eating. In between taking a ferry to Staten Island, climbing to the top of the Statue of Liberty (they did, I didn't), viewing the world from the top of the Empire State Building, wandering through Ellis Island (which Cinelli's father had passed through emigrating from Italy as a boy), and riding double-decker buses from Central Park to the Battery, we celebrated Manhattan by eating.

I am not inclined to drag children into fashionable restaurants. One never knows what a kid might do. Cindy was old enough, and Linda no longer ate with her fingers, but Marty was still a question mark. Once, still in a high chair, he had flung a hot dog into the air at a restaurant probably never intended for children and it had landed with perfect precision between the breasts of a buxom, middle-aged, and very proper woman wearing a very low-cut blouse. She gasped, I sat paralyzed, and the whole room froze until Cinelli, with perfect aplomb, walked over to the lady, said, "Excuse me, I believe that's our hot dog," smiled pleasantly, took the hot dog from the startled woman's décolletage, and returned to our table. I don't think I unparalyzed through the entire dinner. Cinelli should have gotten a standing ovation.

The only glitch in our New York eating experience came in a restaurant on the Upper East Side. We had been visiting a museum, which we did with great frequency, when it began to rain, which it did with great frequency. What to do? Eat. Among the variety of food we managed to consume was steak tartare, which is uncooked ground sirloin mixed with an egg and chopped onions.

"It's a raw animal," Linda said, gasping at the redness of it.

"Well," I said, poking at it, "it's raw and it's steak, so I guess you could say it's a raw animal."

"A *dead* raw animal," Linda added.

Cinelli, the only brave one among us, ate it. I tasted it. The kids wouldn't touch it. Linda did not even want to be in the same room with it. Marty, who had a religious friend back in Oakland, wanted to know if we should pray for it. I was at peace, partially because there aren't many places that can make a martini as artfully as they can in New York. Let the good times roll.

Thunder and lightning over the Big Apple. A subway to the Port Authority bus terminal to get back to North Bergen. Three cops approach. One frisks me. I have a bulge under my raincoat. It's a camera. "Christ," a sergeant says, "I thought it was a cannon. You look like the Hunchback of Notre Dame!" He laughs. The other cops laugh. The kids think it's the funniest thing they've ever seen.

"Is Daddy going to jail?" Marty wonders.

"Fat chance," Cinelli says.

Onward to D.C. We stop at every beef jerky stand, rock stand, Indian artifact store, and snake farm along the way. The two-headed snake impressed us most.

"How does it know what it wants to do?" Marty asked.

The snake-tender looked at him. "I don't know, kid. Ask your pop."

"How does it know what it wants to do?" Marty said again, looking at me.

"You ought to have answers to these questions," I said to the snake-tender, a small, angry man with a chickenhawk face. "That's why we pay you a buck."

"You want your goddamn dollar back?" he demanded.

"No," I said, bristling, "I want to know how the goddamn two-headed snake knows what the hell it wants to do!"

"That's all right," Cinelli said nervously. "We can look it up later."

"I want to know how the hell the goddamn snake knows what it wants to do too!" Marty said.

"Oh, great," Cinelli said to me. "Like father, like son. Maybe all three of you can mix it up. Girls, you want to get in there and kick ass with your father and brother?"

"Cute kid," the snake man said sourly.

"You should be ashamed," Cinelli admonished me as we drove off. "You should know you don't get a herpetologist running a snake stand in an area where fifth-grade educations prevail."

"It's the principle of the thing," I said, feeling foolish.

"You're teaching your son dirty words and violence."

"It's a father's job," I said.

• • •

Barney broke free again, this time in the nation's capital. We were parked not far from the White House, getting ready for a tour, when he slipped the bonds of camperdom and headed up Pennsylvania Avenue. He gave us no warning, no expression or body language, when he was about to dash toward a brief opening in the camper door, flashing from zero to sixty in the blink of an eye. Only when he sensed the opportunity for freedom did he come alive. The rest of the time he either slept or barked.

Off we went again, just like at Niagara Falls, but this time Cinelli stayed with Marty and I led the chase. You have to understand, this was during both the Vietnam War and the cold war, which seems like a contradiction but we managed to make it work. Nuclear missiles were pointed in every direction and we were all as nervous as a Christian Scientist with appendicitis, to quote the musical satirist Tom Lehrer. Richard Nixon was in the White House gathering a team of burglars and bunglers to break into the Democratic Party headquarters in the Watergate Hotel, while overseas we were busy losing the war, which tells you a lot about that era.

It occurred to me as we chased Barney across Freedom Plaza that, given the climate of the times, we could all be shot down as suspected assassins who were urging a carefully trained bomb-carrying dog on toward the White House. The fact that Barney barked all the way and we hollered his name all the way did little to alleviate anyone's fears, but instead called mass attention to our efforts.

Thank God he stopped to sniff a tree somewhere around Pershing Square, possibly sensing the fate of another dog that had headed toward the White House, and I pounced on him. There was a moment as I grabbed his choke chain that I might have been tempted to tighten the chain until his eyes bulged and his bark became a gurgle, but I didn't. Too many people were watching and laughing, and dog murder was probably not the best crime to commit in a crowd. Cindy had thought to bring his leash, so we attached it and dragged him back to the camper, where Cinelli applauded.

So traumatic was the event that I can't remember details of the rest of that Washington stop except that we visited almost everything one visits in the nation's capital and then moved on through the South. We attached Barney's leash to an eye-bolt I installed next to the refrigerator. That did no good in Louisiana. We were camped among the mossy trees near a bayou when the dog slipped out of his choke chain and dashed through an opening. It was early morning and Marty had opened the door a crack to look out when Barney, with the speed of an escape artist, broke for freedom.

I will spare you details of the run. This time Cinelli, still clad in an attractive and sheer nightgown, dashed after him while I unhooked everything and followed in the camper. Cinelli ran, Barney barked, I honked, and here came the crazy folks from California and their damned dog again. Oddly, Barney stopped when he saw the camper. I opened the door and he hopped in as though nothing out of the ordinary had occurred. For a moment, as she glared at him, I thought Cinelli had joined me in wishing the dog somehow incapacitated, maybe a broken leg, but then she thought better of it and we moved on.

I managed to put the camper on its side just outside of Oklahoma City. We were headed for Santa Fe, the sacred place of my mother's memory. It was sleeting and the road was icy. Though barely moving, I suddenly realized I had no control. We were hydroplaning. I somehow managed to slow the bulky vehicle and move it away from a precipice on the right to a dip between lane directions. The camper, at last stopped, plopped on its side. No one was hurt. We scrambled out with the dog barking his fool head off. Cindy brought everyone out from inside the camper, proving that quick thinking does come with growing up.

We spent a few days in Clinton, Oklahoma, where there was absolutely nothing to amuse us but dinner, which, at the only diner within walking distance, was amusing to the point of tears. Pan-fried steak as tough as rhino hide was the specialty. We were lodged in a motel room so small that it made the camper seem like the lobby of the Waldorf-Astoria.

"This," Cindy announced grandly, "is my idea of hell. I used to think Oakland was hell. Now I know it's Clinton, Oklahoma." College gives you that kind of depth and wisdom.

It took all of three days to reset the camper and to reattach it to the back of the pickup. We meanwhile decided that because of the mountains ahead and the worsening weather, we would not go to Santa Fe but instead head south through Texas and on to L.A. My mother was right, I would never get to Santa Fe. The moment sizzled with irony. The monkey-boy fart had failed in his mission.

But oh, what a trip. We saw America up close, not from the distance of a plane but on the ground. And we gloried in its diversity from Harlem to New Orleans, from the precise simplicity of the Amish country to the open plains of Texas, from the bayous of Louisiana to the high mountains of Colorado. We talked to the people of America and heard the music in their speech patterns, the way Walt Whitman once heard it, from the soft, purring drawls of the Mississippi belles to the streetwise dese and dose of the kids in Brooklyn, all contributing to a concerto that plays across the country.

Oh, America.

• • •

We celebrated Thanksgiving in the dining room of a Holiday Inn in Odessa, Texas. It was raining again and they had a fire going in the fireplace. No one else was in the restaurant. Thanksgiving isn't usually a time when you're on the road in a place like Odessa. Families gather. They bring together their sons and daughters and their old people into one home and they thank God that they're them, no matter who they are. They thank Him for what they have, however little.

What we had was much. I thought about this as we sat for dinner. In such a setting, at such a time, one evaluates his treasures. It's another benefit of travel, quantifying personal assets away from the intruding influences of work. This Thanksgiving had a special meaning because it marked a milestone in our lives. I realized anew I had a wife I adored, who was wise and funny and full of tomorrow. Our three children were bright and healthy. Our dog was asleep in our room with no way out. It was a Thanksgiving to remember in many ways, even though the turkey was processed. It didn't matter. Cindy had enchiladas, Linda had a hamburger, and Marty had fried chicken. Cinelli and I, traditionalists in our way, ate the processed turkey with all the processed stuff that goes with it.

It wouldn't be our last Thanksgiving together, but somehow that moment on the road, that rainy night in Odessa, had an impact on my memory few events have had. I remember it as an adventure slowly reaching its conclusion, laughter amid the chaos, new horizons in the distance. I think of the kids growing up, of Cindy in college and Linda accepting a new life on a horse in the mountains surrounding our new home in L.A. I think of Marty being raised in those mountains, attending school, learning to love the outdoors, the small community of Topanga Canyon shaping his future.

When we said good-bye to Odessa, I felt as though we were saying good-bye to our great family adventure. There were miles remaining to L.A., but in the heart of a man sifting through and logging his memories, Odessa was the end. A new world lay ahead.

6

Relatively Speaking

IT WAS MY DRINKING PARTNER Belcher who got me thinking internationally. He had followed me from the *Oakland Tribune* via the *San Francisco Examiner* to the *L.A. Times*. He hated the paper right from the beginning, including its need for long, rambling stories that always began with anecdotal leads. At both the Trib and the Ex he wrote news. Short, hard stuff with news leads that said something right away and didn't amble through gardens of verse to get to the point after the jump. Okay, maybe an occasional feature, at which he was very good, but they were maybe eight hundred words long, not three thousand.

Even though he had stopped drinking at the *Times,* after a transition period from martinis to abstention via white wine, his dour nature had changed very little. He snarled at everyone, and because I was closest to him, he snarled at me the most. But I snarled back, and we managed to coexist on the basis of our common Oakland roots and shared drunken moments. But what irked him the most, for some reason, was that I had never been to Europe.

"Everybody's been to Europe, for Christ's sake," he'd say as we lunched at the Red Dog. "I'm embarrassed to be sitting with someone who's never been to Europe. You mind sitting over there?"

I could handle that once or twice okay, but Belcher was never one to let up. "You'd better get to Europe," he'd say, leaning over the table, "before the gong sounds. We are closer to the gong than we realize." *The gong* was his term for death.

I mentioned to Cinelli that night how close we were to the gong and she said, "That sounds like a Belcher notion. Is he back seeing Ed McMahon again?"

After he quit drinking, the Belch went into depression and was taking a mood-altering drug. When he took it, he fantasized that Johnny Carson's human laugh track, Ed McMahon, was in the room with him. He couldn't stand McMahon because of his jolly nature. Belcher loathed anything jolly.

"No," I said, "he just feels we're not human if we haven't been to Europe."

"Maybe he's right this time."

It was the only time that I can recall her ever agreeing with Belcher. She was for anything having to do with travel.

"You know," she said thoughtfully, "weren't you interested in searching for your family's roots?"

"No," I said.

"Yes. You were. Alex Haley suggested it. I know I'm interested in mine. So let's go hunting!"

Damned Belcher.

Our search for roots began not at an African dig for the bones of man-apes but in Europe, from whence both Cinelli and I sprang. I guess it *was* Alex Haley's idea in the beginning. I was following him around the country on a book-signing tour shortly after *Roots* was published in 1976. In the days when money was showered on us like wedding rice at the *L.A.* by God *Times* (then known for many reasons as the velvet coffin), we traveled freely in order to profile important people, into which category Haley had fallen. In between speeches, he and I were having a drink in Topeka one evening after he'd finished a speech when he said, "You ought to go to Portugal and do your own roots."

I said, "You've got it wrong, Alex. My family consisted of neither slaves nor slave traders from Portugal."

He seemed surprised. "But you are Portuguese."

I had known Haley for twenty years, and I guess he'd always felt I was of the Portuguese persuasion. This is interesting, because when I was hired by the *Times,* the editor, Bill Thomas, also thought I was Portuguese. Martinez is not a Portuguese name. But if the *Times* needed a Portuguese man to fill its ethnic quota, I said okay and viva la Lisbon, or whatever.

Haley said, still mystified, "Well, if you're not Portuguese, what are you?"

"Basque," I said, "and maybe a thimbleful of Mexican on my ne'er-do-well daddy's side. My daughter says we're Basican."

"I'll be damned," Haley said, and then turned to the bartender. "Send us over two more! One for the African and one for the Basican!"

I mentioned Haley's suggestion to Cinelli. She said, "Great, let's go!"

The driveway of our house was rutted, the roof was leaking in new places, and we needed new carpeting. We had no money for a European adventure, however much we might have longed to discover our roots in Italy (for her) and Spain (for me).

"It will be an expedition!" she said, opening map books.

I am not an expedition person. The very word evokes images of tent-camping in subzero weather and portaging one's canoe past roaring rapids and wondering if the chipmunks are rabid.

"We're talking Europe, not Ulan Bator," she argued. "It's time we knew about our antecedents."

"Great God," I said.

They lost our luggage in Milan. Three times we have been to Milan since that first trip and three times they have lost our luggage. "NO *VALIGE,*" I shouted to the man in charge, gesturing broadly. Italians understand shouting and broad gestures. He led us to a room where there were maybe three hundred pieces of luggage. Losing luggage was obviously not new in Milan.

"NOT OURS," I shouted after looking around.

"NOT YOURS?" He turned to Cinelli for confirmation.

"NOT OURS," she assured him.

He nodded solemnly and led us to a window where we filled out forms that included much of our life's history, from birth to that very moment. I expected never to see our luggage again. I would go through Europe unshaved and wearing the same rumpled linen suit in which I had arrived. I looked like a drug dealer from Kuala Lumpur.

"Welcome to our doomed expedition," I said as we drove from the airport in our rented Ford Fiesta. Rain slashed at our windshield. What is it with God that bad weather seems to trail us?

"If Hannibal got over the Alps in a blizzard," Cinelli said, "I guess we can make it through a drizzle wearing yesterday's underwear."

She was born to brave the unknown. Her maternal grandmother's family included the youngest member of the Lewis and Clark expedition, a teenager named George Shannon. I am terrified by the notion that she will want to emulate him and cross the United States on foot someday, living on roots and berries.

It turned out that Alitalia had shipped our bags to Anchorage. I guess in Italian Anchorage must sound a lot like Milan. They were delivered to our hotel two days later and off we went.

We drove toward Santa Lucia looking for relatives of Gus Cinelli. He had immigrated to the U.S. at age twelve pretty much on his own. Reaching adulthood, he married and Cinelli was born. My Cinelli. Then the family broke up and he died. That's like saying *Death of a Salesman* is about an old guy who sells things, has an affair, and dies, but that's the way it's got to be in this instance. Cinelli was raised by a stepfather, the aforementioned Antonio Pinto Ponto Etc., but she wanted to know about the family of her real father. So we went looking for Santa Lucia, a brick-making town in Northern Italy from which Gus had migrated.

What we hadn't known was that there were thirty-six Santa Lucias in Italy and not one of them posted signs that said Welcome to Santa Lucia, the Home of Gus Cinelli or Welcome to Santa Lucia, the City of Bricks. Most of them didn't even say they were Santa Lucia. We learned that from shouting and gesturing with the locals.

Then as we were driving along over paths once trod by Roman soldiers returning from looting and raping, Cinelli said, "Stop!" I hit the brakes, afraid we'd run over something alive. Then she pointed and said, "Bricks!"

"It's a wall, not a factory."

"Turn left!"

She was a woman with a vision. I had to obey. It was like being in the presence of something spiritual. We found a group of people eating outside, communicated our quest, and were led to the home of a woman they thought was named Cinelli. My Cinelli went there on the back of a motor scooter. I followed and waited as they shouted and gestured with a woman in a small house on the edge of town.

When Cinelli returned to the car, she said, "What an odd experience. The woman thought we were asking for someone named Manoli and flew into a rage. She hated Manoli. I'm glad I'm not a Manoli."

A second Santa Lucia yielded similar results. We were directed to a man named Mario in SL2. He knew everyone and in fact had a brother in L.A., which somehow qualified him to lead us to the home of Gus Cinelli. I learned later that almost everyone in Italy has a brother in L.A., and they all own restaurants. He took us to a nightclub that featured German tourists doing the chicken dance. They jumped, flapped their arms, pecked, and squawked until the windows rattled. Hard to believe that people like that almost conquered Europe. During all this, Mario disappeared without doing us any good.

"Maybe the chickens ate him," Cinelli suggested as we drove away.

SL3 was our last Cinelli-roots search. I love Italy, its open countryside and its history-rich cities. I dream of sitting in a sidewalk café in Firenze, a Roman sun warming my face, a glass of chianti warming my soul. But we were running out of time. It took Alex Haley twelve years to discover his roots, but he was a freelancer. I had a regular job, which, alas, did not provide twelve-year vacations.

Our third SL was near Pisa. We stayed in a pension, which is a foreign term for cheap hotel. The owner, Giorgio, hinted that Truman Capote might have stayed there once, but I don't think so. Capote lived in a Manhattan penthouse and buddied around with rich Beautiful People. I somehow doubt he would have lodged in a place with a toilet down the hall.

Giorgio took us everywhere to no avail. No one knew of a Gus Cinelli. It was damaging Giorgio's reputation for knowing everything. He insisted to an old man at a petrol station that he ought to be able to remember Gus Cinelli. The old man insisted he had never known him. Giorgio shook his fist at him and called him *stupido*. The old man in return called him something lyrical in Italian. I suspect it was asshole. That was one tough old man.

That night, Giorgio treated us to a feast at a fish house in town. While I am not opposed to fish, I will not eat just *anything* that swims. For instance, Italians do not believe in dainty fillets. They give you the whole fish, head and all, with eyes that look longingly into yours. And clams. Giorgio brought us a whole tray of clams and said, "Look at this." He pried open a shell and squeezed lemon juice on a clam. It cringed.

"Alive and fresh!" he said proudly.

When he left, I whispered to Cinelli, "I'm not eating anything that cowers."

"It'll hurt his feeling if we don't," she said.

"He can damned well spend the whole night crying. I'm not swallowing food that cringes."

We compromised by putting the clams in a napkin in her purse. Giorgio must have thought we ate the shells too, crazy Americans, but said nothing.

As we left Italy, Cinelli said, "I miss having the kids along. This is our first real vacation without them."

The road wound down through Pisa, San Remo, and the Italian Riviera. A full moon over the leaning tower cast it in gold. The Mediterranean glowed with a light all its own.

"They'd have absorbed it like air," I said. "Even when they fought, they looked."

After our cross-country trip, we had taken one other journey as a family, this one to Hawaii. But, except for Marty, our kids had lives of their own now, working and raising families. Then Marty grew up and left home and there were just the two of us on the road.

"I miss them too," I said.

And we drove silently into the south of France.

Some call it traveler's flu. One gets it quite often at the height of one's enjoyment while struggling exhausted and confused and possibly luggageless through Europe. I got it in Lourdes, the city of miracles. Religious legend has it that a waif named Bernadette saw an image of the Virgin Mary in a grotto there a hundred and fifty years ago, and sick pilgrims have been coming ever since to be cured by touching its stone wall. It is considered a holy place today, similar to a pizzeria in West Hollywood where an unemployed actor claimed to have seen the face of the Virgin in a pepperoni pizza. They called me to verify the vision, but all I saw were tomatoes and sausage slices. The pizzeria closed down, but the actor went on to win a part in the old TV series *Hill Street Blues.* That was another kind of miracle. Even though the pizzeria is gone, the hopeful still cluster at the spot.

Back to Lourdes, where I lay sweating and vomiting. "Why is it," Cinelli said, "that in a place where lepers are made whole and the crippled walk, you get sick? Somebody might be trying to tell you something, Elmer." As she walked away she added, "I wouldn't count on God and Bernadette a whole lot if I were you." She calls me Elmer when annoyance turns to disgust. Sometimes I slur my name, so people think I'm saying Elmer Teenez. I moaned a little louder.

Gift shops, not the grotto, made me whole again. They are jammed along the Rue de Grotto. There's not a lot to do in Lourdes unless you're a leper, so I went crazy on Gift Shop Row. I bought gold-sprayed angels, a beret, bottles of holy water, a walking stick with the Virgin Mary carved in the head, a picture of Jesus with eyes that followed you, and a cup imprinted Count on God. It was my beginning as a gift shop junkie, a condition probably rooted in my genes. Daddy Alfred loved buying ceramic chickens. My mother bought doilies. I bought everything, and it cured me of the flu.

Off to España, humming "Ave Maria."

The Italian and French Rivieras are acluster with small hotels, once you get out of the high-priced districts. Because it was in the fall, we didn't have a lot of trouble finding rooms in small towns, unless there was a big do going on. The hotels were, well, quaint, which is to say small and cheap. Sometimes the bathrooms were down the hall, like the place where Truman Capote may have stayed.

In Monte Carlo, where we didn't stay, we gambled in the large and opulent casino famed as a target of those forever trying to break the bank. Sleek and beautiful jet-setters from around the world gather there, the uber-cool rich who can drop a bundle without flinching. The ones who don't need their roofs repaired or their driveways repaved.

"I feel shabby," I said, looking around at the Dior gowns and the Armani tuxedos.

I was in Levis and a T-shirt that said Real Men Don't Ask Directions. This was not like Las Vegas, where slobbery is considered haute couture.

"You *are* shabby," Cinelli said, "but I'm staying until we break the bank. You can wait at the hot dog stand outside, where shabbiness isn't questioned."

She won $28 U.S. That did not break the bank.

By the time we weathered the Pyrenees and got to the Basque city of San Sebastián on the Atlantic coast, I was ready for luxury. We stayed in a hotel for three hundred dollars a night in a suite with a bathroom larger than our living room. The manager assured us that it was the suite normally occupied by Frank Sinatra. I said, "Show us the records." Cinelli said, "Leave him alone."

In the Basque Country, I was looking for relatives of Leo Larragoite. He was the first of us who came to the New Mexico Territory four generations ago. I began my quest for Leo with the doorman at the hotel. I told him what my project was. He was a large, beefy man with pink cheeks whose only interest in life was to nod, smile, and open the door. He shrugged and said he didn't know any Larragoites. Then he added, "Why don't you just ask around?" That was good enough for me.

"You intend going up and down the Basque coast 'asking around'?" Cinelli said. "You think Alex Haley found Kunta Kinte by 'asking around'?"

"He had his way of searching, I have mine."

At best, it was a sight-seeing venture in an area in love with its past. The Basques are a proud people who cling to the style and architecture of their history. I soaked it all in as I asked around San Sebastián and Bilbao to see if anyone knew a Leo Larragoite. In a taverna overlooking a fishing port, I found three men named Leo, but not one of them was a Larragoite. We bought each other rounds of drinks and had a good time. They spoke no English and I spoke very little Spanish, so we communicated by drinking and laughing. They said Hemingway used to drink there out of long thin martini glasses. I bought a set of six and found myself writing in short declarative sentences. Like this.

The next day I looked in the phone book. There were no Larragoites, but in San Sebastián's old town there was a cabaret owned by a Leo Martinez, ah-ha! I made reservations. Cinelli wanted to know if it was my intention to drink with everyone named Leo in northern Spain. I said, "Who said genealogy was easy?"

Leo's cabaret turned out to be a restaurant. When I informed Leo himself of my heritage, he fixed us a special meal. It began with *chipirones,* which turned out to be squid in its own ink. Add anything served in its own ink to the list of things I will not eat.

"Eat it or leave it," Cinelli said, "I'm not putting it in my purse."

Then he brought cassoulet, which consisted of white beans, garlic, pork, mutton, sausage, and bits of goose. It's what the Basque shepherds ate on cold nights after tending sheep all day. Seeing it, I developed a new eating principle: in addition to not eating anything that cowers or that is served in its own ink, I also do not eat anything with hair on it. The mutton was covered with bristles that were impossible to remove. While their presence may not have offended my rough-and-tumble progenitors, they were not for me. I picked at the entrées, drank raw red wine, and ate hell out of the pastries. Leo Martinez was not related to me.

I guess I never did take the roots thing too seriously. We left the Basque Country without knowing any more about my past than we had when we got there. God knows I asked around enough and drank with enough Leos. Just being there made me want to bomb someone and demand independence. It explains a lot about my instincts. Cinelli says if I didn't have writing as an outlet, I would be running up and down the street throwing hand grenades at innocent passersby. In L.A., it would go unnoticed unless there was a car chase involved.

We headed south toward Madrid, through the snowy Pyrenees. An early winter caught us in the mountains on slick and curvy roads. I drove with the caution of a man who was certain death waited around every icy bend. It was my mother's fault. She hated snow and often warned me about it when I was little. Stories of cannibalism among members of the Donner Party fascinated her. On our way once to Reno from Oakland she said that if I didn't stop jumping around in the car we'd get stranded in the snow and I would end up having to eat my little sister. That thought stayed with me through the Pyrenees. Cinelli took the danger with her usual abandon. Thank God we were out of time and had to go straight to Madrid to catch a plane home or she'd have suggested an off-road trip. We did stop at an enchanting little village one night in the mountains. The men wore berets, the women were lovely, and flowers hung from their verandas; flowers in winter.

This was our first trip to Europe and there was no better way to end it. All through the weeks on the road we were confronted with scenes from picture books that I never thought I'd see in person. But beyond the postcard fronts there were people who were as curious about us as we were about them. We ate in their restaurants, not those adapted toward American tastes, and we slept in their small hotels. We absorbed the cultures and hailed the differences.

The village in the Pyrenees seemed to emerge from the mist like Brigadoon, appearing every one hundred years. The natives brought us fruit and led us to a taverna where a dog that looked faintly like Barney slept in the middle of the room. The memory lingers like a scene from heaven, and someday I'll go back just to see if the village is still there. But next time it will be in the summer.

EVERY WRITER I KNOW *is on an eternal quest for peace amid chaos, a place in the big city where birds sing. I found it in Topanga Canyon. It's a small settlement of about fifteen thousand souls (well, twelve thousand people and maybe three thousand souls) in the Santa Monica Mountains between the ocean and that vast wasteland known as the San Fernando Valley. Once it was the home of Chumash Indians, and then it was the home of outdoorsmen who built cabins and hunted deer, and then the weekend home of big-time Hollywood producers who brought what was known then as starlets to the hills to roll them in the pearlies everlasting, and then the home of musicians and hippies and people who tripped out on acid, and then the home of writers and artists and whispering poets, and finally the home of rich Hollywood producers and lawyers who've built two-million-dollar designer houses that overshadow the more modest abodes of writers and artists and whispering poets.*

We moved there just as the drug era was passing. The few druggies who remained hung around Joe's Market and were called creek rats, but they're just about all gone too. You used to see a lot of hippie buses in town and battered old pickups, but now there are Jaguars and BMWs. State

Highway 27 runs through the center of town and is getting an increasing amount of traffic by commuters who use it as a shortcut home. As a result, there's a traffic signal in Topanga now, which would have been unheard of in the easier days. A lot of the old-timers fought it, but the yuppie lawyers took over.

But everything changes, right? Nothing stays the same in the winds of time that blow through our lives. We have an acre of land where we live and had an old horse for a while named Shorty. It was Linda's horse and she rode it up the trails behind our home into the oak-filled woods. Cindy had stayed in the Bay Area to go to college, and Linda was just about to discover boys and cars, which left poor old Shorty to idle in the makeshift barn that's a carport now. She finally gave him away, and he spent the rest of his days in an open field down in Calabasas, not far away.

Cinelli filled about a quarter of an acre with a garden. She didn't want to come to L.A., but the land that lay waiting to be filled helped change her mind. She's turned the front of our yard into something like an Eden, with stone pathways and clusters of native plants and perennials mixed together in and around fruit trees and towering liquidambar trees whose leaves turn red and gold if a quick frost hits them in the fall. It isn't Vermont in October, but it's ours.

Topanga mornings in the winter are nothing you've ever seen. A mist from the ocean embraces the mountaintops and seeps down into the canyon like ribbons of silver through gaps in the ridgelines. A sweetness born of earth and ocean fills the air, and sometimes, like in the days of El Niño, there are waterfalls cascading down into Topanga Creek.

One can come back to Topanga from abroad, from seeing all the beautiful places in the world, and still be awed by its natural beauty, by its sloping hills, by its paths through chaparral and under oak trees as old as summer. We can live here in peace even as the world churns around us, walking over a Monet bridge in our yard that spans a small creek, to a place under an oak tree that is my Walden Pond. A place to think and to wonder.

I suppose I could stay here forever, watching time alter the nature of Cinelli's garden, growing old in the sweet mornings and the starry nights. But there's just too much world to see. I can always tell when the time has come to board a plane again. I can tell by the look in Cinelli's eyes. I can see the distance. . . .

7

Land of the Sweet Martini

IT WAS AS WE WERE sitting in the shabby, dimly lit waiting room of the airport in Dar es Salaam at 2 A.M. that I began to wonder about our relations with Tanzania. We were six nervous white people clustered together on a wooden bench, being stared at in a not-friendly manner by three Africans across the way. The airport was an old building that smelled faintly of what I imagined to be rhino dung. I turned to Cinelli, who was looking around cheerfully, excited by the new adventure, and whispered, "Where in God's name have you brought me?"

Where indeed.

I have moments when I suddenly realize I've been had, like an old lady who has turned her life savings over to a con man to double her take and suddenly realizes, as she waits for him on a corner, that he is never coming back. My realization took place in an L.A. store called Banana Republic that sold the kinds of clothes one wears on safari. I was buying a jungle hat and pants with a lot of pockets in them when it occurred to me I was going to Africa. As I remembered it, the idea had been broached one evening while I was lying on the couch in my underwear watching a program on the Discovery Channel that featured African lions doing what African lions do best, which is to say, killing, eating, urinating, and copulating. For two months in the rutting season, they fornicate every fifteen minutes. Or maybe it's for two weeks or two days. It is still a feat of manhood rarely achieved among human society, although Charlie Sheen was said to have come close.

Cinelli, who had walked into the room, watched for a few seconds and then said, "It would be fun to go to Africa."

It went by me like a passing cloud. I should have seized on the moment, screamed in fury, and threatened her with a good beating, but instead I said something like "uh-huh" and went on marveling at the length of time a lion can urinate. Before I could say Bwana Jim, I was in Banana Republic buying safari clothes, and then I was in the airport in Dar es Salaam fearing for my life in the hostile environment of angry African warriors. I kept wondering whether us white people had pissed off the third world lately, most particularly Africa, and whether the three men who kept staring at us were among the pissees.

I talked loudly about how Alex Haley was a good friend of mine, figuring that if they liked any American at all it would be him, until Cinelli said, "For God's sake, Elmer, would you shut up?"

We had been dumped at the Tanzania airport after a long flight from Amsterdam and were waiting for our tour guide to take us to Kilimanjaro on the border with Kenya. One of the Africans in the airport was standing behind a bar. When I approached to buy coffee he narrowed his glare directly onto me and said, "No coffee." Then he added somberly, in the tone of a judge pronouncing a death sentence, "You take Coca-Cola." Coca-Cola or you die, kind of. I suppose I could have stood toe to toe with him and said I hated Coca-Cola, but I figured to hell with it, I hadn't wanted to come to Africa to die (in fact, I hadn't wanted to come to Africa at all), so I said, as manly as possible, "OK, Coca-Cola." A shrink had told me to visualize who I wanted to be when in confrontations with frightening people, so I visualized I was Hemingway that time he had come out of the jungle after a plane crash with a woman on one arm and a bunch of bananas over his shoulder. Or maybe it was the bananas in one hand and the woman over his shoulder. Whatever.

The African nodded and shoved out two bottles of Coke, but when I tried to pay with American money he shouted something at me, pulled the bottles away, and shoved back my money. The angry tone of his voice alerted the other two men, who were moving in and talking in loud voices in Swahili. Cinelli, who was watching, said, "You can skip the Coca-Colas, dear." About then our guide came in, a tall, husky African who brushed off the enemy with a few words and shepherded us out to a waiting Land Rover and said, "Welcome to Africa." Yeah, right.

It was in the mid-1980s. I was a columnist for the *L.A.* by God *Times* by then, having been bumped up from feature writing, and the grandfather of a healthy baby boy named Travis, who was Linda's son. Both presented staggering responsibilities and immense potential, which meant I had to stay alive while in Africa. I stressed that to Cinelli so that she would not suddenly want to scale

Mount Kilimanjaro or wrestle a water buffalo, the meanest, worst-tempered animal on God's Catholic earth since the death of an editor I had at the *Oakland Tribune* named Stanley Norton. Up until Stanley's fortunate demise, *he* was the meanest and worst-tempered animal on earth. Just the week before we arrived in Africa, a travel agent was killed by a rogue buffalo, which was okay because there are a lot of travel agents, but there aren't too many newspaper columnists in the world, and there are sure as hell no other Cinellis. So we had to be careful.

What I disliked most about Stanley Norton was his whine. He could whine and roar at the same time, like some kind of demented, possessed baby. But it was effective, and I learned from him to perfect the art of whining to its most magnificent form. Mine is an almost inaudible whine, accompanied by a look so grief-stricken it would make a sailor weep. Cinelli always knows when a whine is coming on, regardless of its subtlety. She says, "Now what?" and tries to make it good for me with a little humor, a kind word, or a threat to smash me in the face. They apply at different times. She, on the other hand, being of the Admiral Farragut Damn the Torpedoes School, rarely whines but is not loathe to declare her unhappiness. Take the brown water episode.

We had just arrived at Tanzania's Lake Manyara Lodge after another ride over roads that had not been improved since the days of Africanthropus, who existed during the Pleistocene epoch, a narrow gap of time between the Ice Age and the invention of the martini. The safari group we were with consisted of tourists from throughout the United States who on the whole were dull but decent people, except for Honey and her man. The lodge, built by the decadent Brits, was on a hill with a stunning view of Africa's distant mountains and rolling plains, a haunting panorama that spoke of time's first dawning. We sat on a veranda having drinks when there was an outburst from a gaunt and sour-faced man named Bud. He reminded me of Horace Redstone in Mexico. Bud was saying, "Honey wants Fanta!"

An African waiter was standing over him, a genteel, soft-spoken man, who addressed Bud in an Africanized Oxford accent. "Sorry, sir," he said, "but we do not have Fanta. We have Pepsi-Cola."

Fanta, for those of you not from Kansas or other places that still drink the stuff, is an orange concoction once popular but now overshadowed by Coke and Pepsi, the fifty-first and fifty-second American states. No one drinks Fanta anymore except in backward places.

"Honey wants Fanta," Bud repeated angrily, to the discomfort of everyone. Honey, his wife, sat smiling dimly and looking off toward a caldera in the distance, as though removed from the conversation. I learned later that *Honey* was not a term of endearment. It was her real name.

"Sorry, sir," the waiter said, bowing slightly. "Pepsi-Cola."

"Honey wants—"

"They don't have no goddamn Fanta!" a large man shouted from another table. He had half risen from his chair, pot-roast–sized fists clenched. I have seen fights before in unusual places over peculiar disagreements, but never in Africa and never over Fanta. "Get her a goddamn Pepsi-Cola!"

Bud, who looked like a stiff wind could blow him over, thought better of the whole thing. He shook Honey out of her coma and stalked off toward his room in the lodge, Honey trailing obediently behind him. Cinelli watched, finished her tea, and said, "What I need is not a Fanta but a hot bath, honey."

She headed for the tub as soon as we reached our room. I could hear water running and, moments later, a shout like the cry of a wounded zebra: "The water's brown!" I rushed in. It was brown all right.

"I'll confirm that," I said. Women need that kind of reassurance. "Take a shower instead."

"It's brown too," she said. "I'm not bathing in anything brown!"

I don't know why the water was brown. I didn't ask. But I wasn't that concerned. While Cinelli cleaned herself with a washrag soaked in bottled drinking water, I showered in brown. I had once gone for a month in Korea without bathing. If crud hadn't killed me, brown water wouldn't.

Adding to the primitive conditions of the lodge, there was limited electricity in our room. The generator was turned on only after dark. The logic was simple: when it's daytime, who needs light?

The lodge was near the Ngorongoro Crater, a volcanic caldera that dwarfs every other caldera on earth. Its upper rim is 12 miles across and its floor is 102 square miles of just about every animal in Africa, except giraffes. The way down to the savannah is steep and forbidding, which convinced the giraffes that it was no place for them. Unfortunately, it convinced neither my wife nor our tour guide, who agreed to a half-hour jeep ride over a nonroad around hairpin turns down to the floor of the caldera, a vast open plane almost six thousand feet above sea level.

I've got to admit thinking back on it that it was an experience. The jeep had a canvas top, but that would have been no protection against the meat-eating animals that surrounded us. We stopped by a half-dozen lions clustered together, dozing in the sun. The guide assured us that there was no danger, their bellies were full, but this brought me no satisfaction as the lion king among them rose slowly and ambled over to the jeep.

I'm not sure how long he stood there looking at us, possibly thinking to himself, like a woman on a diet, that one more bite wouldn't hurt. Time passes at a speed relative to the conditions that exist. We were there only a few moments in a stare-down with the lion, but it seemed like, oh, say an hour and fifteen minutes. I finally said in a tense whisper to the driver, "Haul ass," which was a term he understood, and with some amusement he drove on.

As I look back on the experience, I think of the massive head of the lion, the thick mane, and the puzzled expression on his face. It was another unexpected confrontation with wild nature, the first having been on Mount Rainier, and both probably altered my attitudes somewhat when it came to animal preservation. Cinelli has always had this gentle feeling toward any animal on earth and was overwhelmed by the nearness of the creature, but I've been more zoo-oriented. Now I feel that the free-roaming parks in Africa are where animals ought to be, not in cages too small for their natures.

We ate a chicken lunch by a pond filled with hippos. I felt a little guilty eating chicken as a flock of so-called secretary birds and flamingos watched, but I ate it anyhow, even though it was a member of their species I was devouring. It would be sort of like eating your own cousin. But I was more concerned with the hippos than I was with the birds.

There are all kinds of ways to die in Africa if you're stupid or careless or just plain unlucky. You can be gored by a cape buffalo, attacked by hungry lions who mistake you for a dik-dik, eaten by crocodiles waiting at a river's edge, or bitten in half by hippos. Forget about all those movies starring Stewart Granger and others that depict fatal charges by rhinos. I have a photo of me standing by a rhino and by a park guard armed with a rifle so old it was useful only as a decorative antique. The rifle was to guard against poachers, not wild animals, for man is more to be feared than any beast. Not that I would try to mount a rhino for a ride in the jungle, but I felt at ease with the creature I was standing next to, like Teddy Roosevelt on safari.

Hippos are something else. I don't know how many times I was told how dangerous they could be, especially if there were baby hippos (hiplets?) in the area. Well, there were baby hippos in the area, and their mommies were eyeing us with suspicion. Our guide seemed not to notice at all, chomping away on his chicken leg as though he were in an L.A. mall. I ate faster than I ever had in my life.

"Slow down," Cinelli said. "You get gas when you eat fast."

I hate talking about things like stomach gas in public, but in this case I didn't care. I said, "I'd rather die burping and farting across Africa than die like a bagel in the jaws of one of those things."

The mama hippo made a move that seemed like an aggressive gesture in our direction, and it wasn't lost on Cinelli. She said as casually as possible, "Well, there are other animals to see," and we left. When I looked back, the mama hippo was still staring at us through hostile eyes.

As we bounced away over the road, I said to the guide, "How can you tell a male hippo from a female hippo?"

He replied, "You hold them up by the hind legs and look at their privates."

He laughed like hell all the way up the side of the caldera while monkeys bopped around the boulders and a lion roared down in the savannah. Cinelli just smiled.

We left what Cinelli called the Brown Water Lodge and headed for a rendezvous with a safari group. She had put the whole travel package together with the assistance of an agency that specialized in Africa. We had our own guide for half the time there, and the other half we were part of a safari. The link was a flight from Tanzania to Kenya, a seventy-minute trip aboard a twin-engine Cessna piloted by the Little Dutch Boy. I kid you not, as Jack Paar used to say. He was maybe five-feet-two and had the sweet-faced, pink-cheeked look of a kid about to begin the sixth grade. He was from Amsterdam, we learned later, and in his early thirties. Not to worry.

We got to the plane after a long argument between an immigration agent and our guide. It was in Swahili, so I had no idea what they were shouting about, but at the end it cost me $50 U.S. We walked to the plane parked in an open field and I handed our luggage to the Little Dutch Boy, who I thought was a kid hired by the locals to help out. When I discovered he was a pilot, I wanted to turn and run. It was one thing to be killed by a wild animal in Africa, another to be killed in a plane crash. I could do that anywhere.

The flight was okay except for a sudden unscheduled landing caused by fighter jets that were scrambling in Kenya. It was an exercise, and they'd be headed in our direction, so the Little Dutch Boy decided it would be safer to land than to be in their way. I agreed, with tears of apprehension in my eyes.

"They might shoot us down," the Little Dutch Boy added cheerfully, and then he added with an evil gleam in his Little Dutch Eyes, "like pigeons."

There was another loud argument between the Little Dutch Boy (who spoke amazing Swahili) and some sort of military official, which caused papers to be filled out and another fifty dollars to be paid, but we were on our way again within the hour. Papers are filled out quite often in Africa. I don't know why and I don't know what they do with them, but every time someone demanded papers to be filled, it cost me money.

We were met on the ground by a tall, amiable African named Peter, who was the exact opposite of the Little Dutch Boy. Peter was tall, very dark, and middle-aged, and there was no mistaking him for a baggage boy. He drove a Land Rover that had seen better days, but got us where we were going after a trip that I thought would never end. We vibrated for hours over rippled roads on our way to camp in Meru National Park. When I asked Peter when we would reach the main road he said, "This *is* the main road." Every time we hit a rut, which was often, I bounced through the open roof of the Land Rover. Rut-bounce, rut-bounce, rut-bounce. I felt like an animated creature in a Mickey Mouse cartoon, bobbing down the road and over the horizon.

"I never thought I'd miss the Hollywood Freeway," I said to Cinelli.

She said, "Try not to be tense, dear."

The best way to untense me is to hand me a martini, which is what our safari leader did as soon as we hit camp. Large individual tents had been set up on the edge of a savanna, complete with kerosene lanterns, cots, and a washbasin. Behind each tent was an enclosed canvas shower, into which the Kikuyu tribesmen hired by the safari leader poured hot water. The water was stored in a canvas bag atop the shower, and when you were ready, you pulled a chain and down came the water. I felt slightly decadent having black workers rushing around tending me, but then I thought of the money I'd spent getting to Africa and instantly felt better. I told Cinelli I wouldn't mind having a servant around the house and she said, "You've got one."

Back to the martini. The tables were set with white linen cloths, the glassware was crystal, the place settings bone china, and the utensils sterling silver. If I had to camp, this was the kind of camping I was meant for. It was truly Africa. Across the way, a family of baboons screamed and flashed their red behinds, and far off a lion roared. The sun was setting, painting the sky a glowing crimson, and over the whole ancient land there was a kind of spirituality. I was sinking into an odd feeling of euphoria, until I took my first sip of the martini.

The goddamn thing tasted like strawberry.

"What the hell!" I said, sputtering in the style of an Englishman. I can accept many discomforts during the cocktail hour, including but not limited to baboons that scream and flash their claret posteriors, because they aren't too different in that respect from people in singles bars. But a sweet martini is a true obscenity. To expect a dry martini and get a sweet one is a shock to the human system not unlike kidney failure or a bullet in the brain. It is accompanied by severe nausea, a sudden drop in blood pressure, and an overwhelming sense of betrayal.

The safari leader, Patrick Pape, rushed over, all worried and hand-wringing. A caring and amiable man, he was a combination of Crocodile Dundee and Bishop Edmund Tutu, ready to protect us or pray for us as the need required. When he heard me yell, he thought I'd been bitten by a puff adder, or whatever. We took our sweet-martini complaint to the Kikuyu bartender. He explained that no one had told him what kind of vermouth to buy for my martini, but since Americans ate a lot of ice cream, he assumed sweet vermouth would be the obvious preference. Our travel agent had mentioned before departure that part of the fun of traveling in Africa was the unexpected. I took that to mean that rhinos might skewer a tourist, not that African bartenders wouldn't know a martini from cherries jubilee. I sighed and drank what they gave me.

The late Jerry Belcher would not have been so tolerant in his drinking days. I heard him use curse words once in creative combinations that defied repetition when someone mistakenly gave him a Manhattan instead of a martini. The bartender was so shocked by Belcher's language that he quit and joined a monastery. True story.

Human communication was a general problem throughout both Tanzania and Kenya. For instance: I used to enjoy a cigar occasionally until thirteen million people in L.A. began waving their arms whenever anyone lit up anything, so I quit. I was still smoking them in Africa but ran out. We stopped at a store in Nakuru on our way to a new campsite on the edge of the Masai Mara. At the store, I attempted to communicate my needs to the man in charge.

"Cigar," I said, illustrating what I wanted through wide gestures and grotesque facial movements. I looked like a demented troll.

"See-gar," he said, smiling.

"No," I said, "cigar."

"See-gar."

"Cigar, damn it, man."

He looked worried. "Cigar," he said.

"He thinks you're teaching him English," Cinelli said. "Compliment him."

"Right, cigar," I said. "Very good! You have cigar?"

"Cigar," he said, encouraged.

"Exactly. Do you have one?"

"Sure!" he said, without moving.

"Cigar!"

"Cigar," he said, smiling. But still not moving.

"Give up," Cinelli said.

I sighed. "Good-bye," I said.

"Cigar," he said.

Our new campsite was in a cluster of trees. Safari leader Patrick Pape had never camped in this particular spot before. What he hadn't known was that it belonged to a pride of lions. It was their turf, and lions do not share. This became apparent on our first night. We were sitting around a fire in the burgeoning happy hour dusk drinking strawberry martinis (which now, by the way, are staples in quirky L.A.) when Cinelli said, "What are those little lights?" They were bits of amber in the darkness beyond our campsite.

"Lions," Patrick said cheerfully. "That's their eyes."

"That's a whole bunch of lions," I said. "Maybe nineteen of them."

"How do you know there are nineteen?" Cinelli said.

"I counted eyes and divided by two. Unless there's a one-eyed lion in the bunch, there are nineteen lions."

"Not a *bunch* of lions," a woman from New York said loftily, "but a *pride* of lions."

"Bunch, pride, they'll eat your ass off," I said.

Cinelli whispered, "Don't be crude."

Patrick alerted his Masai camp guards, who observed the amber lights and nodded solemnly. They would protect us.

"Nothing to worry about," Patrick assured us. "No one I know has ever been eaten by a lion."

That night the lions moved in.

"What's that noise?" Cinelli said, shaking me out of a deep sleep.

"It's the pervert in the next tent snoring," I said.

The pervert, a man in his seventies, was accompanied by his daughter, a loud woman who knew everything. Like the couple in Mexico years earlier, it was the kind of arrangement that was suspect. A man and his daughter do not travel together unless one or possibly both are sexual perverts. I suspected the man.

A loud roar split the silence.

"That was no snore," Cinelli said.

Patrick's roar followed immediately. "Everyone stay in your tents! The lions have moved in!"

We peered out the flap. Indeed they had. I am pleased to say my mathematical formula for counting eyes was correct. There were nineteen lions among us. Patrick had started his Land Rover and was attempting to chase them away. They roared and frolicked and ran and returned. Later he would point out that it was a group of teenagers and their mums. The teenagers each weighed about three hundred pounds and, like teenagers everywhere, were quite capable of killing and eating any adult in sight. I had visions of me in a lion's mouth being carried into the bush. An editor at the *L.A.* by God *Times* would say, "What? Eaten by a lion? Did he say anything about his Monday column?"

The Masai warriors, sworn to guard us, ran to the mess tent, but when the lions went to sniff them out, they disappeared into the African darkness, spears and all. Brave warriors in the Zulu tradition they were not. Patrick spent most of the night chasing the beasts in his Land Rover, honking his horn and cursing loudly. Cinelli, an accomplished photographer, wanted to rush out to take pictures, but I clung to her ankles and wouldn't let her leave.

"They're lions, for Christ's sake, woman!"

"They're pictures," she insisted, dragging me to the tent flap.

I held on, and after about an hour, the lions roared off into the jungle, weary of tempting gladiators who wouldn't play. We turned down the lantern and settled on our cots. The light cast soft shadows on the roof of the tent. I was almost asleep when a scream of terror jolted me upright. Cinelli came rolling off her cot, pointing frantically. For a terrible moment I thought of lions or snakes, but then followed the direction of her gesture and saw . . . a spider. It was, at most, a daddy longlegs. To this day, Cinelli swears it was as big as a crab. A king crab. I smashed it into a spot on the tent wall.

"You are willing to go out there with nineteen lions to get pictures, but you're afraid of a spider?"

"Just go to sleep," she said.

The style of gift shopping I had begun in Lourdes, I perfected in Africa. It's called bargaining. Okay, haggling. Normally, I don't haggle when I shop, even in third world countries where there are many fun opportunities for superior Americans to take advantage of the people's poverty and despair. I won't even return defective merchandise. I bought a new shirt recently and when I got home and opened the package, discovered it only had one arm. I am not a one-armed person and don't know any one-armed people, but I kept the shirt because I couldn't stand the idea of arguing with a clerk over how many arms the shirt had when I bought it and what did I do with the other arm.

In Africa, haggling is part of the buying business. Throughout both Kenya and Tanzania, there are small roadside shops that specialize in selling trinkets to tourists, and no price is ever assumed to be final. You bargain. Whenever our convoy of Land Rover and two vans stopped, they'd come running over waving spears, the way their ancestors did when the cursed white man blundered into their territory. But these spears were not intended to skewer anyone. They were for sale. The largest conglomeration of gift shops was in a place on the equator, where one paid to see water swirl backward down a sink. I am told that water normally swirls clockwise down a sink. Here, it was swirling counterclockwise. Big deal.

"We're paying the U.S. equivalent of a dollar to look at water?" I whispered.

"It isn't just the water," Cinelli said.

"Then what is it?"

"It's, well, backward water. The kids would have loved it."

"Yes," I said, remembering their bursts of enthusiasm across America, their giggles and their wonder, "they would have."

Whatever gift shop merchant gets to you in Africa, he inevitably says, "*Jambo, rafiki,* are you from Texas?"

That means, "Hello, friend, are you something other than Japanese?" Texas is a metaphor for the entire United States, which might be an insult, but I'm not sure.

In Africa or anywhere else in the world, there are always more Japanese tourists than any other kind. They tend to move in tight clusters. Cinelli believes it's because they live on those little islands and are packed in from birth. As they grow older and travel, they bind in clusters for comfort. It's in the genes.

Whatever a merchant offers in Africa, he swears he made it himself, whether it's a carved elephant or a shrunken head, although in reality it may have been produced on an assembly line in South Korea or Malaysia.

The first thing you ask is *"Ngapi?"*

Well, I think that's what you ask. *Ngapi* either means "How much?" or "Straight up," I can't remember which. The only Swahili words I'm really certain of are *kwaheri* (good-bye) and *wapi choo* (where's the toilet?).

The haggling begins when he asks for fifteen hundred shillings and you offer him three. He throws his hands to his head, turns away, and moans, as though he is about to break into tears of disbelief.

"No, no, no," he says in great anguish.

You say, "Okay," and begin walking away.

He says, "Wait, *rafiki!*" and then the true bargaining begins.

Cinelli had a formula. She offered 25 percent of the quoted price and bargained upward to 40 percent. If you threw in a T-shirt or a pen, the price got even better. Especially a Texas T-shirt.

My first effort at bargaining was for a walking stick. "Eight hundred shillings," the merchant said.

"One fifty," I replied.

Cinelli overheard. "Your bid is too low," she said. "Offer him four hundred."

"Four hundred," I said.

"Never," he said.

"Walk away," she said.

I walked, the merchant followed.

"Okay," he said, "six hundred."

"Four fifty."

"Five fifty."

"Five hundred. Final offer."

"Okay, okay," he said, "five hundred and your pants."

"My pants?"

I was wearing safari trousers from Banana Republic. He wanted them. I turned questioningly to Cinelli. She shrugged and said, "No one has ever asked for my pants."

I kept my pants and went next door. *"Jambo, rafiki,"* the merchant said. "You from Texas?"

Time was born in Africa. Human time. I sensed that as we wandered through Tanzania and Kenya. There is an elemental nature to the land, a primordial feel. One night, though the sky was clear and the stars were as bright as emeralds, I noticed lighting striking a mountaintop in the distance.

"It's always there," Patrick said pleasantly. "Like God had chosen that place to show his power."

It was always there, all right, every night, striking that mountain-top, God or not, like a mad scientist, relentless in his quest to blast life into existence at that one place. Did early man emerge from just such power and chaos, a microbe born in fire that grew to walk and think and sing songs to himself under the moonlit sky? I mean, hey, Patrick could have been right, who knows? What better way than lightning flashing out of darkness, glowing briefly in the distance, searing into the retina, to show power?

Africa grows on you, becomes a part of not just your memory but your soul. African offers depths of feelings never before explored. I can see it now if I close my eyes. I can smell it, hear it, feel it. Africa.

MAKING FRIENDS WHILE TRAVELING *is like gathering daisies at the end of summer. Ultimately the poor things are going to die and you're going to toss them into a garbage can and forget that you ever picked them. Same with people you meet on the road. Sometimes you even mean it when you swear you'll keep in touch with the couple from Ocracoke, North Carolina, or Plano, Texas, but that kind of sincerity is usually created during a long cocktail hour in a country where you don't know anyone anyhow. I generally have nothing in common with people I meet when I'm drinking in some forgotten place, and it's just as well they're forgotten. They were dear friends for about half a beat, and now they're back on the farm.*

Patrick Pape was different. There was something special about the guy, a pink-cheeked Brit who was as much a part of Africa as the lions that roamed the tall, dry grasses of the golden savannas. He understood the sounds and smells of the bush and knew every rut in the dirt roads that led to secret places. He was born in Kenya to farmer parents who had survived the Mau Mau years and who had learned to live with the animals that roamed free. He grew up to lead safaris through the plains and forests he had roamed as a child, respectful of the teeth and claws of the jungle's predators, but never afraid of them.

Getting to know him during our weeks with his safari, I began wondering how a man so soft-spoken and gentle could be so integral a part of an environment that existed on a cycle of predator and prey, where death could be so savage and sudden. But I eventually came to understand that he considered himself a guest in the kingdom of the lion, and his deference was a sign of homage to the free-flowing life that surrounded him.

Uncharacteristically, I kept in touch with him over the next few years, and when I heard he was coming to the U.S. on a tour to drum up business for his safari, we invited him to our home. Civilization terrified him. He had only been out of Africa twice before in his forty-eight years on trips to the U.K., and he couldn't get away fast enough. A man who could chase wild animals from an encampment with the aplomb of a child taking a slipper from a kitten had suddenly met his match with a garbage disposal.

When Cinelli turned it on after dinner, he swung around like a man under attack by crocodiles, staring at the sink from which the growl of the disposal had emerged. It took a moment of calming and a lot of laughter to convince him that a garbage disposal is a lot less lethal than a pride of lions prowling one's encampment.

The second time he came to America encompassed the kind of love story that operas are created to tell, intertwining need, loneliness, sudden romance, and tragedy. He had been divorced not too many years before and had just discovered he had skin cancer. It was a lonely and worrisome time for him, until he met Susan Brenneman, a woman of culture who had once soloed for the San Diego Master Chorale. She too was coming away from the end of a long marriage.

Susan had gone on safari with her brother, a Southern California physician, and his wife, a surgical nurse, "to get away from it all." One of their stops was a camp led by Patrick. There was instant rapport between the willowy blonde and the gentle bushman. She made him laugh. He made her love Africa the way he did, with depth and meaning. Their romance bloomed in the soft African nights. When Patrick told them of his cancer and the lack of any medical insurance, the brother offered to arrange free treatment in the U.S. if he could get there on his own. He could stay with them during the procedure.

Patrick did manage to save enough again to fly to the U.S. and to their home in Laguna Beach, on a cliff overlooking the Pacific. A team of experts did what they could for Patrick, and the prognosis seemed good. He and Susan were married in the home of her brother. It was a fairy-tale union to which Cinelli and I were invited, a ceremony performed on a veranda over the pounding surf. They were as radiant as teenagers. They returned to Africa together, but the magic of their relationship, of finding each other in the wild, free domain of Kenya, was not to last.

Patrick's cancer returned, and now it was attacking his brain. He returned to the United States one last time to be told there was nothing that could be done to save him. He accepted the awful verdict with the same grace and equanimity that characterized his confrontation with lions. We met them for dinner in Long Beach, just before his return to Africa. He wanted to die there. The pain he was feeling never marred our last visit. Cancer never darkened his gentle spirit. As we parted for the last time, he said, with a smile—a smile!—"Well, I'll see you in heaven."

Patrick died some months later. If there's a heaven, I'm sure it's a place where giraffes glide by beyond the forest, where herds of elephants lumber down trails flattened by their massive footsteps, and where the amber eyes of lions speckle the night. And I know Patrick is there.

He was one friend from the road that we kept until the end. He was still on our minds when, a short time after he died, we emerged from a shroud of sadness and reached once more for the distance. This time, Germany.

8

Long Memories

GERMANY HAUNTS MY GENERATION. I was a child when the Second World War broke out, and grew through my teens with news of war's victories and horrors. In my young adulthood and into middle age, Germany's division into East and West was a symbol of the cold war, locking the world into two hostile and dangerous camps. Deutschland's contemporary history shrouded my life. We had to visit this nation that had burned its indelible mark on the twentieth century.

We were in Berlin by accident when the reunification of Germany occurred. It was one of our wandering trips through the parts of Europe we hadn't seen. Cinelli loves it when we just rent a car and hit the road. I favor a more organized approach to adventure, but what the hell. I go along because I'm a husband and that's what husbands do best. We go along.

Our timing into Berlin was spooky. We stumbled onto history with no planning on our part. East and West partied at the Brandenburg Gate. We saw the faces of the young, glowing with hope, and the faces of the old, dark with memory. A million people gathered on the night of October 3. Vendors selling beer, flags, and sausages made fortunes. Communist sentries, standing guard on a wall overlooking the Unter den Linden, gazed nervously over the noisy festivities, but it was a night of celebration, not violence. After forty-five years of divided rule, the two Germanys were one.

Those who spotted us as Americans bought us beer and knockwurst sandwiches. We waved the black, red, and gold flag of the German Republic, a paper replica that is now a part of my workroom clutter, a reminder of what the world once was and could be again. As we cheered with the crowd to the noisy oompah music of a German band and watched fireworks light the night, an older German standing next to us said in English, "I wonder what will happen now?" We all did.

John Updike wrote in the *New Yorker* that history begins where memory ends. We're still in the memory phase of the Second World War, of Hitler leading this nation of Bach and Einstein into a catastrophic confrontation with the rest of the world. People will ask someday how this could have happened, allowing a madman to declare such a dark future. They will ask how the people of a cultured and civilized nation could have followed that stupid and ugly psychopath, that charismatic thug, toward destruction.

One afternoon during "teatime" in Berlin, when Germans take time off to enjoy lush pastries and rich ice cream, we sat at a table with a woman whose husband was an industrialist. Unlike America, in Europe you share tables if there's a vacant chair, without feeling as though you're invading anyone's privacy. There is no territorial imperative over there when it comes to tables, no ferocious protection of one's space. Even the same bathroom is shared by men and women, although the stalls are properly divided. It takes a little getting used to, realizing there's a half-naked woman on the other side, but necessity requires that one adapt quickly, and I did. Walk into a women's room in L.A., and a cop will club you into bloody submission. Over there, it's no big deal.

In a conversation that lasted for an hour, I asked the teatime woman, a tall, regal Berliner in her sixties, how the German people could have followed Hitler when it became so apparent what was happening. The question encompassed not only the war but the mandate of the "final solution" that resulted in the worst case of genocide in human history. She thought for a long time, her fork suspended above her plate, the segment of chocolate éclair on it assuming an almost surreal presence.

One can only guess what must have been going through her head. Guilt? Excuses? Apologies? Explanations? Around us, conversations were noisy and animated. Waitresses wearing frilly aprons bustled about in the crowded restaurant. Outside, along the busy Kurfürstendamm, a mixture of cars and double-decker buses rolled by, all the busier because of the feeling of celebration in the air.

She was frozen in thought for several moments. Then, just as I was about to press for an answer, she set down the fork without eating that final bite, put money next to her plate, and stood. I remember her expression. It wasn't sad or angry. It was blank. There was no animation to her features, no response to either my words or my presence. Was the memory too hard to face, the question too difficult to answer? She simply said, "I'm sorry," and disappeared into the holiday crowds. I watched her leave, and I wondered.

The trip to Germany began in Helsinki, Finland. We were a curiosity there, waiting for a connecting flight to Oslo. I don't recall staring at foreigners in our airports with such intensity. We just kind of glance up at whoever passes and go back to eating our Twinkies. In Helsinki, it was Dar es Salaam all over again.

"Isn't this a Communist country?" Cinelli asked, responding uneasily to the Finnish stares.

"I think so," I said. "I'm not sure who is and who isn't these days. It was so easy once. Bad guys, good guys, no in-betweens. You're either for me or agin me."

"I'd hate to end up in one of those gulags," she said.

"I don't think they have gulags here. But don't be intimidated," I said, feeling intimidated. "We're Americans. Stare back harder! Jump into their faces!"

"It's that kind of thinking that's gotten us into trouble for two hundred years."

"Well, then, just think of them as inferior and avoid them."

We had plenty of time to avoid them. Takeoff was four hours late. At twenty-eight thousand feet, the captain came on the PA system to explain that the reason the flight had been delayed was that three of the plane's four hydraulic systems had failed just before boarding and had to be fixed. I would just as soon not have known that. He sounded like a contractor we had once, whose name was Ollie. Ollie's idea of repairing any construction goof was to slap a little paint on it. A crack discovered in a support essential to holding the house up? Slap a little paint on it. A floor that's sagging? Slap a little paint on it. Three of four hydraulic systems on the verge of failing in flight? Slap a little paint on them? I prayed not.

But we made it, and our rented Volvo was waiting for us. So was the hotel. It never ceases to amaze me when things go right. It is best to expect the worst when traveling. Schedules go to hell, borders close, cars break down, hotels suddenly go out of business, or someone declares war on someone else. You learn to ride with the bad and enjoy the good.

What I remember most about Oslo was the Kon Tiki Museum. There in glorious form was the balsa raft that had ferried Thor Heyerdahl 4,300 miles in 101 days from Peru to Polynesia. He and the five other Scandinavians that accompanied him on the 1947 trip were attempting to demonstrate that the South Pacific Islands may have been settled by ancient Peruvian Indians using rafts similar to the *Kon Tiki*, which was named after a Peruvian sun god.

Even though Heyerdahl's trip was a success, he never did convince anyone that his theory was valid. He did, however, write a book that fired the imaginations of kids everywhere in the postwar world, including this kid. I was in high school when the book came out, and I immediately went to the San Francisco office of Aramco, the Arabian-American Oil Company, and applied for a job with Standard Oil in Saudi Arabia. I'm not sure how I connected a job in the oil fields with the trip of the *Kon Tiki*, but it seemed reasonable at the time. Fortunately, I was turned down because I was too young and because I lacked any of the skills required to pump crude oil from the ground.

Oslo never seemed that interesting to me except for the Kon Tiki Museum and cocktails at the Palace, where it is said the playwright/poet Henrik Ibsen used to drink several glasses of aquavit, an aperitif flavored with caraway seeds. Anyplace Ibsen drank was good enough for me, except that I am emotionally incapable of drinking anything flavored with caraway seeds.

It was late September and the skies were constantly overcast, except in the mall, where it was always summer. It was there I bought my finest trinkets. But first I had to pay for them, and that wasn't easy. Because we were traveling to several different countries, each with its own monetary system, I had begun the trip carrying only traveler's checks in U.S. dollars. At one shop in the Oslo mall, don't ask me why, they took only German deutsche marks. So the dollars had to be changed into deutsche marks and then into Norwegian kroner. I am certain that during the transaction, I was screwed out of several dollars or deutsche marks or kroner, but there was no way for me to know. I have a handheld calculator that will do the work for me, but it takes more time than anyone is willing to give. I got so confused in a taxi in Rome that the frustrated driver grabbed the wad of lire from my hand, took a bunch of it, and handed me back the remainder.

I was happy to leave Oslo because it reminded me too much of Oakland, and, in fact, with about a half-million people it was about the size of My Old Home Town. I can't think of Oslo without thinking of what Gertrude Stein said about Oakland, that there was no there there. Maybe there was some there there, but not so's I noticed.

We drove our Volvo from Norway into Sweden, where we took a ferry into Frederikshavn, Denmark. It was just an overnight in Sweden in a dank upstairs room at the Savoy Hotel for 685 kroner. That translated into $125 U.S. I suspect that Europe has two sets of prices, one for them and one for us. *'Ere comes a Yank, it's up the old kazoo!* But that's just part of traveling, I suppose, and of being a rich, hated, used Americano.

"I know you're disappointed in leaving Sweden," Cinelli said as we ferried across the Kattegat toward Denmark, "but we'll be back. Then you can walk into the lady's vagina."

"You'll never let me forget that, will you?"

"You've never stopped talking about it. Just walk right in there, take a seat, and look around. Maybe stroll up the vulva or the clitoris after a while."

I read about a display in Sweden that dealt with procreation. They had a giant vagina and you could walk in and discover how babies were born. I already knew that, of course, but the idea of a giant vagina . . . well, you know.

She sighed. "If only you had a giant . . ."

"Enough!"

They had no giant vagina in Denmark. But they did have a glorious green countryside that a couple could wander through and not suddenly have to get onto the Hollywood Freeway. But even meandering, we were still slightly disoriented. We had never fully adjusted to the time in Europe. Jet lag screwed up our bodily fluids so badly that we were never sure whether we were eating breakfast or dinner, so we ate a lot at breakfast in case it was dinner. We also had strange dreams, especially Cinelli. She told me one morning, or maybe it was afternoon, that she had dreamed she had three children, two named Thurman and one named Truman. I dreamed I was being forced by a talking dog to retire on March 27. The dog didn't say why or of what year. I said, "Make me a buyout offer, dog!"

Ribe. That's a town, not a Mexican beer. In fact, it's the oldest town in Denmark, located in roughly the center of the country, between Brorup and Billund, if that tells you anything. It made sense to Cinelli, who can decipher any map. Ribe is over eleven hundred years old and was once home to the Vikings, whose depictions you may have seen in old movies. Kirk Douglas as Eric the Red, although I think we just called him Eric the Viking or the Bold or something during the cold war.

We stayed in the Dagmar, which was built in 1581 and is Denmark's oldest hotel. Everything is old and quaint and cobblestoned in Ribe, which under normal circumstances might become excessive, except that it's a beautiful little town, more or less restored to what it was back then when Eric took his ale at the Dagmar. Or his grog, maybe. I'm not sure what Vikings drank.

It rains a good deal in Denmark, which is why it's so green and fresh. One can even breathe the air without fear of black lung or dry mouth, which is a new experience for a guy from L.A. (I keep thinking of Bob Hope's line, "I'm not breathing anything I can't see.") With no industries in the area, no abundance of cars, and no coal-burning homes that I know of, this is a place of another time. Its centerpiece is a towering, nine-hundred-year-old cathedral with 248 stairs that one can take to the very top. Cinelli took them, but I don't do stairs to the top. An escalator, maybe, an elevator for sure.

Ribe is actually the name of a river that runs through and in some places under the town, tumbling over waterwheels into a widening waterway. I guess there was an outlet to the North Sea, since the Vikings did more than sail up and down the Ribe looking for new lands to conquer, and maybe to loot and pillage. Conquering Brerup and Billund over and over again would seem a limiting adventure.

Cobblestones and quaint half-timbered homes can get a little old after a while, but the Old Lamplighter was something else.

"Will you quit calling him that," Cinelli says when I talk about him. "He wasn't the Old Lamplighter. He was the Old Town Watchman. And you both drank too much!"

It's a ritual in Ribe that the Old T.W. comes around every night in his period costume, holding a lamp and a pole topped with a spiked ball. During the tourist season, which September is not, because it rains a lot, he is followed by a parade of people with still and video cameras, like the Pied Piper of Hamelin leading the rats into the sea. He was more casual during our visit, sauntering through the Dagmar's dining room, where he talked a little about the town and its folklore.

His visit caught us in mid-dinner, after I'd had a martini or two, which encouraged me to wave him over for a drink. He was a pink-faced man with the kind of jolly look required of a guy willing to walk around in a funny costume, cadging drinks and telling stories. I'm a big spender after two martinis, so I ordered over a sixty-five-dollar bottle of Pouilly-Fumé, which I graciously shared with the Old Lamplighter while Cinelli shook her head. But by then, both the Old Lamplighter and I were beyond the effects of head-shake admonitions, so we drank, toasting America and Denmark, and had one hell of a good time. Only the next day, as I paid the hotel bill, did I become aware that the dinner had cost $176 U.S.

It was, as one might imagine, a tensely silent ride through the lush countryside of Denmark, its greenery glistening like emeralds in a soft rain. I knew that if I said anything at all, even offering how beautiful it all was in my sweetest tone, I would bring down on my head a storm of unpleasantness, so I hummed quietly and drove and tried not to think of my pounding headache. Goddamned Old Lamplighter.

We entered Germany in the late afternoon and stayed in a bed and breakfast in a town called Plön. Even the name was boring. Absolutely no one spoke English in Plön, and they probably only spoke a lower form of German, the way Cajuns or people from Mississippi have their own primitive languages based roughly on English. It was the first time we'd encountered this. Usually *someone* in town was able to speak a little American, but not in Plön.

This became terribly apparent in a restaurant we stopped in that night in what was regarded locally, I'm sure, as the town square. It was the only eating place open, and it was jammed. A waitress the size of a sumo wrestler and with the personality of a rottweiler pointed to indicate that she wanted us to sit at a table occupied by another couple, who were about as uncomfortable as we were. I had the feeling, however, that had we refused to occupy that table, Frau Homicide would have come at us with a meat cleaver. The people at the table were nice enough, but, like the rest of Plön, spoke not one word of English. You'd think that they'd have seen one of our movies and at least be able to say "You talking to me? You talking . . . you talking to *me*?" like Robert DeNiro in *Taxi Driver*. We all made a valiant effort to communicate, but it was an exercise in futility.

When it came time to eat, there was no way to determine what the menu said. We carried a little yellow book called *Langenscheidts Universal-Worterbuch* that was supposed to translate "Englisch to Deutsch" and visa versa, but we couldn't do it fast enough to please Frau Homicide. However, since everyone seemed to be eating sausages, I pointed at a sausage-eater, pointed to Cinelli, and pointed to myself to indicate that both of us wanted sausages. I added an explanatory word, "That!" and pointed to the sausage itself. This not only provided a moment of entertainment for those in the restaurant but got us our sausages, huge things with mounds of sauerkraut and potatoes.

It was the only thing interesting in Plön.

Lübeck was next. It rises abruptly out of the ordinary, a medieval city of towers and spires that dates back to the twelfth century. Hard by the river Trave, it's so damned picturesque you want to eat it, like one of those gingerbread houses Grandma gave you. Count Adolf II of Holstein, a formidable name, founded Lübeck in 1143, although it had already been a settlement for a while. Notable in its more recent history is the fact that on March 29, 1942, it was the target of the first bomb attack on a German city in the Second World War. About a fifth of the old town was destroyed.

One enters it through a massive gate that tells you immediately you're driving into history. It also told us we were almost out of cash. It was a revelation that hit us as we started looking around for a place to stay. By this point in the trip, we were beginning to realize that if we kept spending at the current rate, we would have to sell the house, the car, the dog, and one of the cats in order to maintain a certain standard of living when we got home. That standard of living, while minimal, did include eating and sleeping in our own beds. So we decided to find a cheap place to stay while in Lübeck. I mean, how comfortable could they have been eight hundred years ago? A modest hotel would do just fine.

I'm not sure how I found the place that seemed to cater to winos and drifters. It was off the main street, which is always a good sign, and its simple exterior was in sharp contrast to the Gothic nature of the rest of the town. I was met at the front desk by a man who responded to my cheerful *"Guten Tag"* with a silent glare. I thought it meant "Good afternoon," but judging by his hostility it could have meant, "I'm going to cut your dirty Nazi throat."

I said, very slowly and loudly, "I would like a room. Do you have a room? A room. Do you have a room? I-would-like-a-room." He pushed a book at me and said, "Sixty deutsche marks." I was going to suggest that I'd like to look at the room first, but since we only had seventy-six deutsche marks left, there was little incentive to quibble. I signed the register and we brought the luggage in. That is, I brought my luggage in. Cinelli took one look at the room, turned around, and walked back to the car.

"What?" I said, as she sat in the car, arms folded, staring straight ahead.

"It's a flophouse," she said, "and I'll be damned if I'll stay there."

"But I've already paid him."

"Then I'll get the money back."

I don't know what she did, but she marched back into the place and returned triumphantly a few minutes later with our sixty deutsche marks. We went on to find a hotel that accepted traveler's checks, paid about four times more for the room, but at least didn't have to lie down with winos.

"Did you really expect me to sleep in that place? It was like that motel in hell."

She was talking about that motel near Grand Rapids that had turned out to be a place frequented by outlaw bikers. They partied all night and kept stomping up and down the exterior hallway, yowling and roaring like great apes. I don't know that great apes actually yowl and roar, but drunken bikers do. About midnight, Cinelli demanded that I go to their room next door and tell them to shut the hell up. I explained that would be tantamount to shaking my fist at a great white shark, and she said if I was too chicken to do it, she would.

Just about then, there was a loud thud and a scream, followed shortly thereafter by sirens and then by motorcycles revving up and then by silence.

"Thank God," I said. "They've killed somebody and left."

I don't know if they actually did, but no one bothered us for the rest of the night, and we were out of there at dawn.

The hotel in Lübeck that we finally settled for was a dream compared with the flophouse I almost got us. The room was kind of pink and frilly with a lot of bric-a-brac trimming and porcelain figurines. The bed was so high, one had to hurl oneself upward like a high jumper in order to achieve height enough to land on it. But we slept well. For the next couple of days, we visited cathedrals, museums, a street where the writer Thomas Mann may or may not have walked, and an empty rococo hall that had once been the party pad of Herr Somebody of Somewhere. We oohed and aahed over the various gingerbread buildings, found good places to eat, rode a paddleboat on the Trave River, and then went onward toward Berlin. I realize that's a quick summary of a city founded in the twelfth century, but that's what you do when you tour. You simplify.

We entered what was then East Germany somewhere around a town called Ludwigslust, past an abandoned guard tower once manned by Communist soldiers who'd just as soon have shot you dead as looked at you. Remnants of barbed wire remained, but the gate was wide open. It took us down a rutted road littered with abandoned Russian-built cars and into a city as silent and dreary as a ghost town.

The contrast between East and West was never clearer than in Ludwigslust, where empty stores stared out through dust-stained windows onto desolate, deserted streets. We had driven through countryside in West Germany that was immaculate, on roads that were as perfect as any in the U.S. We had shopped in stores filled with all the necessities, and most of the luxuries, of life. Here was failed totalitarianism side by side with a free society, and if there was ever a doubt in anyone's mind which was more desirable, he only had to visit Ludwigslust.

But then, Germany has always been a land of contrasts, of Hitler and Einstein, of music and terror. We wondered as we drove how a people that generally seemed so amiable, so helpful to strangers, so intelligent, could be lured by a madman into a war that killed millions. How could this nation of thinkers put to death six million other human beings because, in effect, they didn't like them? These are questions asked among the nightmares. We would ask them later on a cold, bleak day standing in the empty prison yard at Buchenwald.

After a few days in Berlin, with its new East-West unity, its massive celebration, and its deep foreboding about the future, we headed for Prague, the City of a Thousand Spires. It was fiesta time there too. We arrived, of course, in the rain, and the hotels were full. Our only option was to drive back through the storm toward the border with Germany and search the darkness. It was almost midnight. The towns we passed were dark. There were no hotels.

"Why is it," I asked, "that every goddamn time we take a vacation, there's a goddamn fiesta going on?"

"We got a room in Berlin, didn't we? And that was one *biiiig* fiesta," Cinelli said. "So stop complaining and stop swearing and stop right there, I see someone!"

It was a town with no name. None of the towns had names, and most had no people on the streets. This town had two humans walking along in the rain. While they didn't speak English, a form of international communication is a look of desperation and the single word *hotel* shouted loudly. "Ah-ha," the man said and pointed.

We found a building with a red sign that said Park Hotel, but it was no park. Studying a map later, we decided we'd been in a town called Teplice, just south of the border with what, up until the day before, had been East Germany. On the main floor was a brightly lighted restaurant loaded with drunken Red Army soldiers. I mean falling-down drunk. Whether they were celebrating or sorrowing we had no idea.

"Oh, good, a restaurant!" Cinelli said, peeking in.

She is often oblivious to danger. I am not. While she might say, "Oh, good, a tiger shark!" out of a scuba diver's curiosity, I would get out of the water as fast as I could, dragging her with me.

"Good, *hell*," I said, pulling her away from the dust-streaked window before she was seen by the drunken soldiers. "That's the Evil Empire in there!"

The lobby of the hotel, if you can call it that, was up a dark stairway to a second floor landing. I rang a bell, and an empty counter was soon filled by a large, hairy man in a ribbed undershirt, picking his teeth and glaring. He belonged to that subspecies of primate with arms longer than its legs and an inability to communicate beyond grunts and monosyllabic words. I couldn't imagine that his ancestors had been walking upright too long.

"What?" he demanded abruptly, chewing the last bites of something. I dared not speculate what. Later we would refer to him as Igor.

"We'd like a room," I said. I almost added, "I think," but didn't. It was late and we were tired.

He demanded our passports. This was a procedure required by many hotels at the time, but this one bothered me. I had a vision of us being hauled off to a Siberian Gulag because we didn't have passports, living on cold, bug-filled porridge, fighting off cockroaches and rats and—

"Room 321," he growled, slapping a key down on the counter. We backed off.

It was more of a cell than a room, possibly six feet by ten feet at the most. There was no elevator in the building, so we hauled our luggage up three flights of stairs to what the Red Army must have considered luxurious accommodations. The room consisted of two cots, a small sink, one chair, and a cracked mirror. The toilet and a single shower were across the hall.

"I'm going to shower," Cinelli said.

I grabbed her arm. "You are not going to appear nude in this hell house!" I said.

116

"I'm going to shower, not walk up and down the hall naked."

"No way! This place is filled with drunken, horny soldiers! I know what that's like! I was a drunken, horny Marine once, remember?"

"I'll die here of dirt and starvation," she said, flopping back on a cot.

"There are better ways to die," I said, "than at the hands of a plundering army."

"I don't really think they're plundering," she said. "Igor would never allow it."

The sun was shining as we entered Prague, but the hotels were still full. After about the tenth "No room," a cabdriver saw us emerging from a hotel, read our forlorn-American expressions, and said he knew where there was a room. He asked Cinelli to jump in the cab with him and I was to follow in the rented car. Now that I think about it, I'm not sure why she was to ride with him. But mine is not to question why when you're married to a pretty woman. We got a room at the Centrum Hotel for fifty dollars a night. It wasn't exactly five-star. Maybe no-star. But it was clean, it was cheap, the room was large, and the toilet worked. We asked so little.

Born in the thirteenth century, Prague has maintained much of its early appearance, with its spires and squares and ancient buildings. It's a small jewel in our memory, eye candy for the soul. There is much to see in Prague. It's not a big city, but its museums, art galleries, palaces, and monuments are endless. Its churches and palaces comprise the spires of this pretty city, a picture on a postcard with the Vltava River winding through it. Only a group of pickpocketing Gypsies marred our visit. They surrounded us in Old Town Square, created a noise that would shatter eardrums, and began hugging and pawing us. I knew what was going on and shouted for Cinelli to beat them off.

She thought they were just locals who loved us, but I knew they were thieves. I began whacking at them the way rich landowners must have once beaten the peons, and they came away pretty much empty-handed except for a pair of my glasses whipped out of a shirt pocket.

"You were sure pounding those poor people," Cinelli said as the Gypsies drifted off to find another mark.

"I know," I said. "It felt good. I haven't beaten anything for a long time. I miss the dog."

Getting lost is a way of life on foreign roads. I don't know how many midcity roundabouts I circled, unable to determine the correct outlet to take and unable to take it if I wanted to. They're like whirlpools, spinning cars around in endless circles until they are either flung out of the automotive eddy by centrifugal force or drawn down into the depths of the pool, never to be seen again.

Almost every foreign country we've ever visited has roundabouts, but almost worse than these endlessly circling configurations of traffic was the highway reconstruction program of newly united Germany. The day after East and West were rejoined, workers of the West were out fixing the deteriorated autobahn system in the East. This included that section of the road out of Eisenach.

We went to Eisenach in the first place because composer Johann Sebastian Bach was born here. One of our daughters married a Bach, and while one may argue that his musical abilities are less than Johann's, he does play a pretty good guitar. This is also the town in which Martin Luther began his translation of the Bible and precipitated the Protestant Reformation. Raised a little hell, you might say.

After one visits the Bach Museum and the Lutherhaus, where young Martin lived as a schoolboy, there's not a lot else to see. We stayed in a hotel that had also once housed Russian soldiers, but it must have been for officers only because the rooms were larger. It did not, however, hold a candle to the Intercontinental Hotel in Gera.

The Intercon, as they called it, offered about as much luxury as East Germany could afford, but no one was in the hotel to enjoy it. The lobby was empty and most of the rooms unoccupied. Dining was formal in a large room with gleaming chandeliers and tuxedoed waiters who hovered around us like crows, because there was no one else to serve. We ate off expensive china and drank from crystal glasses. The eating utensils were sterling silver, and the place settings were something out of a royal banquet. To match all this splendor, the food was on a gourmet level. We felt as though we were staying at the Ritz, and I suppose in East Germany, we were.

That Eisenach seemed to lack anything close to the Intercontinental was quite all right with Cinelli, although I looked back in longing. However, the real problem wasn't the living conditions in the hometown of Bach, but how in the hell to get out of it. The freeways, or autobahns, were closed off in many sections while the West Germans went at them as if they were rebuilding the pyramids. One big difference between Communism and Capitalism is that we have better roads, and the West Germans wanted to live up to that. The only problem was, we felt trapped in Eisenach.

Cinelli was reading the map and had figured out our way back to the autobahn, but we couldn't get there. A policeman stood guard at its entryway and was directing traffic onto a side street with the abrupt and annoyed manner that has characterized cops since the beginning of time. We had a more difficult time than usual understanding him. It's always annoying when foreign people don't speak American, but then most American cops also have a hard time with the language, so what did we expect abroad?

We drove down the street that he indicated by pointing and making guttural sounds, meandered for an hour, and ended up back where we had begun. Same intersection, same cop. We tried once more to pry directions out of him and thought we had come up with the right way to go. Wrong. For the third time we arrived back at the starting place, like game pieces being jiggled around on a playing board.

By now, he knew who we were, a couple of American idiots who couldn't find their own assholes in the dark. He began raising his voice in a manner reminiscent of Hitler addressing a crowd from the steps of the Bundestag. "Freeway kaput!" he screamed in the only American he knew. Intimidated, we set off again. I realized as we circled the town once more that we were passing the same austere-looking brownstone building that we had passed three times before. Judging from words we could pick up off a sign, it seemed to be the local mental hospital. One more time around and we were both certain the cop we kept meeting at the intersection of our nightmares would throw us into one of its padded cells.

"I'm not going back to that guy again," I said. "He already hates the very sight of us. No telling what he might do."

"I think you're right," Cinelli said. "Head that way."

We wandered a bit more, past the imposing Wartburg Castle glaring down from a hillside, and valleys so green they blinded the eye. Somehow we broke into freedom and ended up on the autobahn at last, glad to leave the dreaded cop of Eisenach to our rear.

We reached Buchenwald by feel out of Weimar. There are no signs that direct one to the first of Germany's notorious concentration camps. It wasn't listed in our tourist books. What was left of the camp that once held twenty thousand tortured souls at a time sat in a wooded area about five miles northwest of Weimar, home of the

Republic whose collapse opened the door for Hitler. Buchenwald was a work camp and there were no gas chambers, but hundreds of Jews and other prisoners died every month from disease, malnutrition, exhaustion, beatings, and executions. Experiments were performed on the prisoners to test the effects of vaccines and viral infections.

The cold, gray day matched the mood of the camp. An icy wind whistled through tall pines. Dark skies lowered over the barbed wire. A monument that memorialized those who died there seemed small and insignificant. You wanted more. A museum and library were closed the day we were there. But we wandered the grounds, looked into the remaining buildings, and tried to imagine what it must have been like for the crimeless prisoners incarcerated there. It's a haunted place, iced by both wind and memory. I could almost feel the presence of those who suffered under the swastika for the mad vision of Germany's demented dictator. In Weimar, in a café not far from the camp, we were easily spotted as tourists when we stopped for coffee. No one spoke to us, which was unusual. Gazes were averted. They knew where we had been, and a great guilt overlaid the moment.

Why come to a place like Buchenwald, so bleak, so cold, so awful? Because history demands it. What transpired is never erasable. The best we can do is learn from the past to build monuments of humanity over the graves of savagery. And to store in our collective memory what we are capable of doing to each other.

When we left, Cinelli looked up the road that led to the camp. "How could they have done that?" she asked. There were tears in her voice. The question hovered, unanswered, in the dark autumn day.

9

Where Hell Froze Over

I DON'T KNOW WHY rain seemed to follow wherever we went. We were rained upon in Mexico, in Africa, in various campsites on the West Coast, all across the U.S. and in other places I'll mention as we go along. The coldest rain was in Alaska. We had flown to Barrow for no other reason than because it was there, the most northern city in the U.S., unheard of until the Trans-Alaska Pipeline opened in 1977. It originates near Barrow and stretches eight hundred miles to Valdez, an ice-free port on Prince William Sound, where it is warmer, but not considerably so.

Cinelli said, "Wouldn't it be fun to go to Barrow?"

I said, "No."

She said, "I'll bet nobody goes to Barrow."

I said, "Exactly."

"It would be tourist-free."

"For good reason."

"It's a place of beauty and adventure."

"It is also the place where Will Rogers was killed in a plane crash. I am not going anywhere where a humorist was killed."

"That's it?"

"That's it."

Click your heels three times, blink your eyes once, say no eight more times, and presto, you're in Barrow. I don't remember doing all that, but I do remember being in Barrow.

It is a windswept place on the Beaufort Sea, north of the Arctic Circle. Strong men have died there, I'm sure, mushing across the frozen tundra, fantasizing that they were in Hawaii, stripping off their clothes in the hallucination-created sunshine, and perishing in the bitter cold. Polar bears ate them, growling over the final frozen remains.

"I'm sorry," the desk clerk said at the Top of the World Motel, "you're not in the book."

She was an unpleasant woman with a clipped manner of speaking and a nasty way of licking her lips. Under normal circumstances, licking one's lips can denote a pleasurable experience or a sexual lure. In Martha's case (a badge she wore over a fur-lined jacket said Martha Welcomes You to Barrow), it was simply disgusting. Even Cinelli, who is without a critical bone in her body, was put off by the constant licking. "She's like a dog," she said later.

"I have reservations," I said impatiently. "I personally made them for three days, starting today. Check your book again."

She licked her lips, scanned several pages of the book again, and then slammed it shut. It was a large book, a precomputer-age book, and when she slammed it, a cold breeze puffed into my face.

"Not here," she said.

Our son Marty, now a teenager, and his friend Troy were with us. They stood by a stuffed, eight-foot-tall polar bear that dominated the small lobby. Worried expressions crossed their faces.

"In your book or not," I said, "we're here, so find us a room."

"Sorry," Martha said, licking, "we're full."

At the time, the Top of the World Motel was the only public accommodation in the ugly little town. There was a large supermarket, two restaurants, a nameless coffee shop, and a Mexican eatery called Pepe's. The rest of the town was composed of the airport, an Eskimo or Aleut meeting hall, and several ramshackle homes. I couldn't tell an Aleut from an Eskimo, but that wasn't my problem at the moment.

"Listen to me carefully, Martha," I said, leaning over the counter. "The last flight of Alaska Airlines has left Barrow. We have no place to stay. I made reservations here. Now either you find us a room or we will sleep naked in your lobby huddled up next to your Goddamned polar bear. *Capisce?*"

I don't know that Martha had ever been threatened before. She licked her lips frantically and flipped through the book again. "I've got a small one," she said.

It was smaller than small. Two single beds that barely fit in the room and a bathroom too small to adequately sit in. On the toilet, that is. In order to sit, the door had to be left ajar to make room for one's legs.

If Cindy and Linda had been with us, we'd have had to sleep stacked. But with lives of their own, they had opted out of the Barrow trip.

"This is repulsive," Marty said, utilizing a newly discovered word. "I'm not sitting on the can with the door open."

"Excellent," Troy said, meaning, one assumes, that Marty was right, it was repulsive.

We brought Troy with us to keep Marty company. His father was an itinerant surfer who, when he wasn't surfing, walked around with a coffee cup half filled with scotch. To the best of my knowledge, he was either surfing or drinking. *Excellent* and *dude* were the surfer words of that era. The extension of the little and index fingers, shaken briefly, was the symbol of the day, meaning "Hang ten, dude." Hanging ten indicated ten toes over the forward edge of a surfboard. If, however, due to accident or whim of nature, one possessed only nine toes, I suppose it would have been "Hang nine, dude."

Surfers surf no matter what the weather conditions. During the violent storms of El Niño, when hillsides slid and houses were swept away, surfers challenged waves off L.A.'s beaches that were taller than goalposts. During sewage treatment plant breakdowns, of which there seem to be many in L.A., they surf in the effluence that spills into the ocean. Not even a little floating fecal matter or the kind of bacteria that eat horses damps the zest of the Malibu boys for the waves. Cinelli sees them as affluence among the effluence.

We took the bed by the window, which looked out at the compelling beauty of an iceberg-filled sea, gleaming chunks of blinding white hills floating on the pure blue of the ocean. Colors flash into memory with a computer's speed, each in deep contrast to the other, startling dichotomies that characterize this strange and frozen world. Our room, by contrast, was overheated, but just looking at the cold blue water and the gleaming chunks of ice made us cold. We took the window bed because in order to reach it, one had to crawl over the other bed. I didn't want anyone crawling over me. We crawled over them. It was like being in a lair of snakes, all slithered together, entwined and overlapping. But it was home.

. . .

There was no real public transportation in Barrow, only a single taxi operated by a sallow-faced man with sunken cheeks, a pockmarked face, and shifty eyes, all of the physical characteristics generally associated with serious felons. I'm sure he did hard time somewhere for murdering his mother and twin sister and mutilating their bodies, and then killing and eating the family dog.

He shared with us once how much he hated Barrow, Alaska, Eskimos, taxis, seal meat, elk steaks, television, tourists, and things I have since blocked from my memory. He hated them all. We were forced to endure the man after trudging about a mile through snow to the aforementioned coffee shop. It was bitterly cold, and rain was beginning to fall, accompanied by an icy fog. This was in July, when in the civilized world the sun was shining and little children were running through lawn sprinklers.

"We're going to die out here," Marty said. He never has been given to a lot of emotionalism, unlike Cindy and Linda. This was a declaration of fact as far as he was concerned. We *were* going to die out there.

"This is excellent," Troy added as we slogged forward, the partially frozen ocean to our left, nothing either ahead or behind or to our right. I'm not sure whether Troy meant that he liked or disliked what was transpiring, but I can't imagine him thinking it was good.

"Mart is right," I said to Cinelli, trying to catch my breath in the severe cold. "We will die out here. Time and a thousand snowfalls will cover us, and our frozen corpses will be discovered a million years from now, like Piltdown Man."

"Keep walking," she said. After a moment she added, "There was no Piltdown Man. He was a fake. The bones were animal bones. Keep walking."

"You don't know everything."

"I know you'll never be Piltdown Man."

"Why are we arguing archaeology on the brink of death?"

"It's better not to think about death. Hum 'Nearer My God to Thee' and step out briskly."

We were heads down into the cold, slogging toward where we thought the coffee shop was when a slurred voice said, "Whaddayadung," or something like that. An Eskimo or an Aleut staggered into our midst, breathed his whiskey-soaked breath into our faces, and, without further preamble, tried to hug Cinelli.

"Hey," I said, shoving him away, "you don't just walk up and hug people."

He muttered something equally unintelligible and tried to hug me.

"Get the hell away!" I shouted as the boys stared.

"Maybe you shouldn't anger him," Marty said.

Before I could respond, the Eskimo (or Aleut) staggered off into the icy fog.

"There goes humanity's next discovery in a million years," Marty said.

"Excellent."

"Feel sorry for him," Cinelli said. "Alcoholism is a terrible problem among the native Alaskans."

"It was a terrible problem in Oakland too," I said, "but we didn't go around hugging everyone."

"Oh, yes you did."

I felt like Stanley finding Livingston when we found the coffee shop, a decent place that served huge hamburgers, which we devoured like starving huskies. I had been dieting severely before our trip in a futile effort to attain the thin look that was all the rage in Los Angeles. There are no fat people in L.A., at least not in the daytime. Perhaps they come out at night when their obesity is not as apparent and the risk of being stopped and beaten by thin people not as great. My mother had cursed me with a potbelly and my father with short legs, so fully accomplishing The Look was a goal I would never achieve. As a columnist for one of the largest newspapers in America, I felt I ought to present a body that was at least not a double for Porky Pig's, and tried to eat pickingly. It didn't work, but I don't care anymore. I have pretty much decided that I don't want to die in L.A. either, unless they improve their attitude toward potbellied people.

In the bitter cold of Barrow's summer, I came to believe I should build up fat if I wanted to survive, and therefore ate like a polar bear about to hibernate. I devoured two thick hamburgers and every french fry that came with them. I was like a dingo dog ripping apart a jackrabbit, even though there are no dingo dogs in Alaska.

When it was time to leave, a look out the door convinced us that, as Marty had predicted, a frozen death awaited or, as Cinelli put it, lethal popsicleization. The icy fog had moved in for real and the rain was falling harder. I don't know why it wasn't snow. I guess you could call it sleet, but I think it was something, well, wetter than that. You couldn't see much beyond the edge of the coffee shop's porch, so thick was the fog that clutched the tiny building in an evil embrace. That's when the waitress told us about the taxi, which she called for us.

The misanthrope at the wheel drove blindly through the fog and rain while informing us of his many, far-reaching, and all-inclusive hatreds. The mile from the restaurant to the Top of the World Motel was filled with them.

"I've hated snow since the day I was born," he said in a voice as flat as steel. "All the goddamn sleds and skis."

"They can be a nuisance all right," I said, for lack of anything better to offer. I was next to him in the front seat and felt it my obligation, as a way of protecting the family, to make conversation, however limited. A man's got to do what a man's got to do.

"Fucking, no-good snow," he said.

"Bastard," I added.

There was no road, and visibility was zero, but the Hater made no effort to ease up on the accelerator, slipping and sliding on a route that edged the deadly sea.

"This is it," I could hear Marty whisper.

"I think so," Cinelli said, surprisingly gloomy. She is rarely that way, which reinforced everyone's notion that Marty was probably right.

Despite our misgivings, however, we did reach the motel. The short trip cost nineteen dollars. It was outrageous and highway robbery and a lot of other rotten things, but I gave him a twenty-dollar bill and was just glad to be alive. I wasn't about to challenge a guy who had killed his mother and twin sister and then eaten their dog.

"We learned a lot about hatred from that guy," Cinelli said, as we crammed into our small room. "All about the fucking snow."

"Excellent," Troy said.

The sun eventually came out, but the icy wind off the Beaufort Sea continued. I had never been that cold before, not in Korea, not in Milwaukee, not anywhere. If someone had said to me, "Go to hell," I would have replied, "Fine, send me there, close to the fires." If damnation was warm, I was for it.

For the remainder of our trip, we shivered through short walks to the Eskimo (or Aleut) Center, past racks of drying seal meat, and were entertained by native children who took turns bouncing one another into the air on blankets held at each of four corners by other native children.

Both Marty and Troy wanted to try it but were informed that it was some kind of sacred ritual that could not be shared with outsiders. I insulted them by offering them money to ignore their sacred ritual and let the kids bounce, which also offended Cinelli.

"Do you also offer to buy pork chops for Jews on Yom Kippur?" she demanded as we left the building. "Or maybe you spike the holy water at Saint Joe's and drink it right out of the bowl. That's cute, Elmer, real cute, offering money for them to deny their Gods. No wonder they hate us."

We ate at Pepe's on the last night of our stay in Barrow, surrounded by a team of black basketball players. I wanted to ask where they were from and why in the hell they were there, but didn't. Instead we ate our tacos and refried beans, which were about as expensive as dining at the L'Hermitage in Beverly Hills, and flew into Anchorage the next day. It was thirty-eight degrees there, and young men without shirts were playing football on a half-frozen field. We stayed at the Captain Cook Hotel, turned up the heat, and ordered room service.

Alaska is the Africa of America. It has the same primitive feel, the same elemental geography. Nature dominates in Alaska the way animals dominate the Dark Continent. There is a massiveness to the snowy mountains, a feeling of isolation when you're in the midst of these gleaming-white peaks. Alaska is a visual world, and we absorb what we see to reconsider it years later. Everyone should go to Alaska.

We did tourist things after Barrow in the vicinity of Anchorage and Fairbanks, but even so one can still hear the voice that called and continues to call inhabitants to this unique and sprawling state. On a small fishing boat in Prince William Sound, later polluted by a massive oil spill, there was a silence one rarely feels, a stillness to the cold air that permeates to one's inner core.

We could see bald eagles along the shore, perched on the high branches of leafless trees, very much like the proud American symbol they represent. Killer whales played in these icy blue waters, and the skipper of the boat, a man who had fished the Alaskan coast for thirty years, spoke of these giant, intelligent creatures as though they were puppies on a leash.

I'm not sure why I have to be dragged to these wondrous places. Perhaps I am very close to the beast, straying from my territory only during times of famine, and returning when the herds of wildebeests finally come back to be eaten.

"I'm surprised you don't mark your turf by urinating against a bush," Cinelli once said to me.

I leaned in close. "What makes you think I haven't?"

"Don't touch me," she said.

TICK, TICK, TICK . . .

It was Satchel Paige, the quintessential baseball philosopher, who said, "Don't look back, something may be gaining on you." What was gaining on me was time. The gap between pursued and pursuer tightens as one ages, until the slap of death's sneakers on the pavement becomes louder and more persistent and then, whammo, he's got you.

I became aware of this relentless pursuit by the passage of lives, the deaths of those whose existence intersected with mine. Harry Lehman, the brutal, son-of-a-bitching stepfather of my youth, was the first to go. I didn't mourn him. He faded over a period of years from the angry, erect, teutonic devil that he'd been into a sad, frail old man with a puzzled, mournful expression, as though he were being physically squeezed by the relentless pressures of time but had no idea what was happening to him.

A three-pack-a-day man, Harry died of emphysema. My strongest memory of him in those last days is of a wizened victim struggling for breath in a hospital bed in Oakland's V.A. Hospital, as pale as the walls that surrounded him. The last thing he ever said to me was, "It won't be long now." I wanted to reply with something comforting, because anger and vengeance have no place at an old man's passing, but I couldn't. I just looked at him. He died the next day.

Daddy Alfred was the next of the parental trio to go, the hard-drinking, fun-loving hero of World War I, whose last ceramic chicken still lives in our kitchen, a cookie jar filled with rubber bands. He used to say he wanted to die in bed with a strange woman at his side and rosary beads in his hands. As far as anyone knows, one part of his wish was answered. He died in bed.

He was managing a seedy hotel in downtown Oakland frequented by old men on pensions when I got to know him again. He had written to me in Korea but made no effort to contact me later until he showed up one day in the lobby of the Oakland Tribune. *His hotel was just a few blocks away. He had seen my byline in the Trib and decided that now was the time we should get together.*

My mother kicked him out when I was five, so I have only fleeting memories of him in my life prior to our meeting in Oakland. The sharpest picture is one of him and Harry Lehman fist-fighting in our front yard, and me standing nearby, watching and crying. And then he disappeared.

Daddy Alfred wasn't a big man, but there was something big about him. His laugh was large, his enthusiasm was large, his drinking binges were endless, and his love for our kids, his grandchildren, immense. I was startled to see him at the Trib. He stood there for a moment looking and smiling, carrying a shopping bag filled with ceramics, and saying nothing. Then he bellowed, "Alfredito!" and embraced me in a bear hug the crush of which even a real bear would be hard-pressed to match.

We talked for an hour in the lobby and then for another hour across the street at the Hollow Leg, the Trib staff's favorite eating and drinking place. He wanted to know all about the Korean War and talked about his war, the war in which he had won the Silver Star, that war to make the world safe for democracy, the war to end all wars. His medal hangs in my room; and the citation for bravery, as faded as the memories of those battles a long time ago, is in a metal box nearby.

He didn't drink that day, but he still drank a lot. It was binge drinking. He'd stay sober for two years and then stay drunk for three weeks, day and night, until he emerged so sick and drained that he swore he'd never touch another drop, but he did.

I guess I could understand why my mother couldn't tolerate him. Seeing him made me temper my own drinking habits. Maybe that's the best a bad father can do is to set a lousy example for his kids not to follow. I think that in his fading years he realized how he had failed me and tried to make amends. I see him as he was in the weeks before his death, jovial to bursting, laughing loudly, eating grandly, then disappearing into drunkenness and finally death. He was eighty.

The ceramic chicken, the medal, and the flag that draped his coffin are all that I have of him. There is a photograph of their marriage, Mary and the irrepressible Alfred, but my mother had cut out his face.

Death claimed her next, the enigmatic Mary, who traveled the open roads she could afford and rarely looked back; not a great mother but an enduring character, and a storyteller par excellence. Or maybe a liar. Lying in its extrapolated sense is a form of storytelling, I suppose, if we're discussing fiction. She couldn't walk to the store without returning with tales of dragons and strange figures in dark doorways and the secret flutter of wings in the night sky.

On the other hand, she had developed The Lie, that estrangement from the truth that colored her entire personality, storytelling aside. She had learned to lie in her youth, I would guess, to cover her hell-raising episodes, whatever they might have been, and then she had to lie to bill collectors and later to those who wondered why Harry Lehman was living at our house. While shacking up is no longer a subject of gossip and *condemnation, it was back then, so Mary decided that Harry would be her brother and my uncle. Forget that there was absolutely no resemblance, no family traits whatsover, he was still my uncle, despite snickers to the contrary.*

My mother felt the distance in her soul even as we feel it today, Cinelli and I. She never stopped making bus trips to Reno, even near the close of her life when walking was difficult and money scarce.

A bunch of old ladies would rent a single room and take turns sleeping, in between playing the nickle slots. Mary, seeking to beat the odds, stayed up all night playing and slept on the bus heading home. She won twelve hundred dollars once and never ceased talking about it. That was her trip back to Santa Fe, she'd say, a journey home again. But she never made it. At age seventy-six, sitting in an easy chair at my sister's home watching television, she suddenly began babbling in Spanish, a language she had almost forgotten since childhood, talking to the ghosts in her head. It was a last conscious act before a stroke crippled her brain. She died a few days later, never having regained consciousness.

But there's a strange addendum here that I still think about years later. I was holding my mother's hand as she lay on her hospital bed. When my sister Emily asked if she was happy, my mother, deep in a coma on the last day of her life, squeezed my hand firmly three times in a signal Emily had arranged earlier. Wherever she was, Mary was indeed happy. I was hoping that by the measure of her own private heaven, she was in Santa Fe. It was her Mecca. Paris is mine.

10

Anywhere but Bombay

PARIS BELONGS TO LOVERS and dreamers. Old people from Ogden, Utah, with sour stomachs and a tendency to wear matching leisure suits, should never go to Paris. It is not for the timid or for those who limit their budgets or for those who never wonder what's at the other end of an allée.

We did not go only to Paris on this trip, but to Madrid and London and Vienna too, but it is Paris that endures as the city of my memory. I see it as we linger over lunch in the Eiffel Tower as a storm passes over the rooftops, dressing the dark afternoon with flashes of lightning, drumming the day with thunder. There it is. Rain again. My mother used to say I was born in a storm, and maybe I was, because thunder follows me.

But like elements of great music, percussion defines beauty too, and it all went together to form an enduring image of a city I've seen now a half-dozen times in varying shades of glory, but never as glorious as that first time.

Our trip began in London. This tour of Europe was not Cinelli's first choice. She wanted India. It is not enough for this adventure-minded woman to dine in the finest restaurants of Europe, or even the more interesting restaurants of Europe, and to stroll the ancient streets. There must be, well, tigers in her life. There must be something different.

"India is different, all right," I said, as we faced each other over plans for our next trip. "You can die of a cold in India. There's bacteria everywhere. In the air, in the water, in the food, in the air vents, in the buses and the trains, crawling up from the toilet. And"—I added, allowing a tone of disgust and repugnance to creep into my voice—"there are filthy little monkeys everywhere."

"What in the hell," she said, "are you talking about?"

I get most of my information from television. I saw one of those travel documentaries about a village in India where monkeys were considered sacred. As a result, they flourished. There were monkeys on roofs, in the streets, in the trees, running up and down the street, scurrying through grocery stores, stealing food off fruit carts, sneaking in open windows, polluting with their stinking urine and defecation where they went, the nasty little buggers.

Cinelli stared at me.

"I always suspected you might be bipolar," she said. "Now I'm sure of it."

"I saw it! It was a veritable monkey-fucking village! Not only that"—I leaned closer—"India is rife with cobras. Thousands of tourists are killed each year by cobras. Diseases are spread by sacred cows. Mules with open sores on their bodies—"

"Stop, stop," she said. "I've heard enough of your idiocy!"

She began leaving the room and I said . . .

"Spiders."

She stopped. Among the few moving creatures that Cinelli is leery about, spiders top the list. The Japanese ran a close second for a while due to the World War II Slap-the-Jap propaganda that was showered upon us and the macho nature of their society, but I think she's over that. Spiders she will never get over.

"Now tell me you saw one of those History Channel things on spiders in India."

I could smell her fear.

"They're as big as plates," I said. I had no idea if that was true. "And they kill more people than cobras or monkey disease combined." I'm sure that's probably not true. "I have an idea."

"What's your idea?"

"Six words. The Great Art Museums of the World."

"That's seven words."

I could see she was interested. Art is a passion with her. She is a volunteer at both the L.A. County Museum of Art and at the spectacular hilltop Getty Center. She knows more about art than many artists.

"Think of the Louvre, the Tate, the Prado and . . . whatever else."

"What's your plan?"

"An art tour."

Bingo.

The idea was to go cheap. It is always our initial thought. We swore once that we could tour California from one end of the state to the other on practically nothing. We would stay in accommodations on the level of Motel 6, or Motel 3 if they existed. Motel 2? Why not. We would eat Corn Flakes for breakfast and carry bread and cheese for lunch. At night, dinner would be off the cut-rate senior menu at Denny's. A little of this, a little of that. No martinis, no wine, no *foie de veau* or *baba au rhum*. A burger and coffee will do just fine. And maybe a glazed donut, but not every night.

It was on the California trip that we came to realize we are emotionally incapable of going cheap. It was our wedding anniversary, so we stayed in a three-star hotel in San Diego and celebrated at a four-star French restaurant. Then we bought a fifteen-hundred-dollar oil painting at a gallery in upscale oceanside La Jolla, dumped the bread and cheese, and went crazy. The car broke down just south of Eureka and we said to hell with it. It was old and bothersome, so we bought a new one. By the time we returned to L.A., we had seen California on two thousand dollars a day. It was not a budget trip.

To save money on the art trip to Europe, we flew across the U.S. both coming and going on airlines I had never heard of. I was grateful that the transatlantic lines had familiar names, although I supposed it wouldn't make much difference whether our plane plunged out of the sky into water or onto a grassy meadow. When the drop is thirty thousand feet, you're history either way.

One of the airlines was Kiwi Air. While unaccustomed to flying on airlines named after a fruit, I was pleased to observe that the wings didn't flap and the crew seemed sober. Aboard an Air Transit Airlines jet on the second leg of our flight to New York, I was startled when one of the customers suddenly reached out and patted a stewardess's behind, and she just smiled and kept going. I thought at first it might be a kind of ATA good luck tradition, but the stewardess, sensing my interest, explained that the man was her husband and not simply a frequent flier with special privileges.

• • •

We made side trips in the U.S. before heading for Europe. Our first was at the Chicago Art Institute, where I was introduced to Claude Monet. Lines to view the exhibit went halfway around the block, and we were informed that we had to have reservations to even think about getting in.

"You were supposed to look into this," Cinelli said. "Show them your press credentials."

Press credentials can be a two-edged sword. For whatever reason, there are seasons during which everyone is encouraged to hate the media. There are other seasons, however, when the magic of the First Amendment flickers through the sky like Tinker Bell, and us guys in the media suddenly become saviors of the American Dream.

I think that at the time of the Chicago Monet exhibit there was public outcry over the fact that porn dealers on the Internet were also using the First Amendment to protect their right to advertise "teenage pussy" and "sluts doing everything with animals." As you might imagine, this did not, and still doesn't, sit well with the good churchgoing folks of America, and so the term *media* was not, and currently is not, in the Tinker Bell stage.

At any rate, I returned to Cinelli without a reservation to the Monet exhibit.

"Did you show them your police credentials too?" she asked, frustrated by my failure.

"I showed them everything but the tattoo of a butterfly on my ass," I said, "and it did no good."

"You don't have a tattoo on your ass."

"Whatever."

I don't know exactly how it happened or what she did, but she strode off and returned in a few minutes with two tickets to the

140

exhibit, go right in, have a nice time, bye-bye. When I asked what kind of spell she cast, she replied mysteriously, "It's the international sisterhood of art museums."

Hmmm.

I loved Monet and his water lilies and hay stacks and dabs of color, but I did not love Claes Oldenburg, who was one of the modern artists featured at New York's Guggenheim Museum of Art. He was, however, good training for what was to come when we reached Europe.

"I don't know what you'd call this," I said, looking at the depiction of a giant, half-eaten apple core formed out of foam rubber and canvas, "but if this is art, I'm Modigliani."

"I'm sorry it isn't a little boy by a fishing hole," Cinelli replied, "but I'm pleased that you could pronounce Modigliani. One thing at a time."

For those unfamiliar with Oldenburg, he had made a handsome living creating oversized, really BIG replicas of familiar things, like the aforementioned apple core, plus a light socket, a toothbrush, a hamburger, a windshield wiper, and other "soft sculptures" representative of the pop art movement.

But at least he wasn't disgusting. Mapplethorpe was. His exhibit of doctored photographs posing as art was bracketed by signs that said, "Please be advised that viewers may find the photographs in this exhibit disturbing."

Well, yes.

While Jesus as a crucified chimp might not upset you, how about a guy pounding a nail into his nose? A woman breast-feeding an eel? A mixture of fresh fruit and animal guts? Old ladies with their heads sliced open and their brains spilling out? No. Wait. That was by someone named Joel Peter Witkin, but done in the same style as

Mapplethorpe, if indeed any kind of style was involved. Probably a close friend.

I woke up disoriented in a London hotel, the Forte Crest, dreaming I was a boxing writer covering a murder trial involving Rocky Balboa. The room was dim, and when I looked out the window the day was dim too. I didn't know if it was early in the morning or early in the evening. For a terrible moment, I thought I might be in hell.

Cinelli sat up in bed, her eyes filled with sleep. "What's the matter? You look like someone took your adjectives away."

"Are we in hell?"

"Is the British Museum nearby?"

I looked out the window. "Yes, I can see it!"

"Then we're in London."

Jet lag. The changes in time flying back and forth across oceans and datelines throw my brain and my body into varying conditions of psychological dishabille. I'm wide awake at three in the morning and sleepy at five in the afternoon. I think it's Tuesday when it's Wednesday. Not that that makes a huge difference. Tuesday and Wednesday are not significant days.

But not knowing the correct time of day does make a difference. Waking up at 3 A.M. and thinking about going out for a martini is detrimental to the human condition. Well, not just thinking about it, I guess, but actually doing it, which, thank God, I never did. It's the idea that's scary. Not until several days have passed in a new country do I begin to adjust to the local hour. Then it's practically time to move back to the U.S. and start all over again. But since London is always kind of dim, even if you know the correct time, you aren't sure. That's why Jack the Ripper went so crazy.

. . .

Back to the art tour. I was introduced to the cartoons of Agostino Carracci in London's National Gallery at an exhibit called "Gods in Love." Before you begin wondering what kind of cartoons might have existed three hundred years ago, let me assure you we are not talking Snoopy or Donald Duck here. Cartoons in those days were preliminary drawings that were ultimately transferred to the ceilings of cathedrals and castles.

"I know you were expecting Pogo," Cinelli said, sympathizing, "but you'll just have to settle for Cephalus and Aurora."

She was talking about the painting in which Cephalus, the mortal husband of Procris, is carried off by Aurora, goddess of the dawn, while her own aged husband, Tithonus, sleeps. Curled up nearby while all this is going on is Tithonus's dog, who just stares but doesn't utter a single bark. Barney was like that. He only barked when it was inappropriate. Otherwise, silence. Gods and goddesses could empty every room in our house and Barney would just stare dumbly without making a sound. Only when silence was essential, like for illness in the house or a sleeping baby, would he bark his face off.

I am not an art person. I can understand nudes, gods, and visions of hell, but the modern stuff falls under the category of doodling. I recall staring at an abstract painting by one Vanessa Bell that consisted of a series of multicolored squares. I wondered as I stared at it what Bell had started out to do and how she knew she'd done it.

"That is the visual equivalent of Shakespeare writing 'To be, to be, to be, to be' over and over again without expanding on the possibilities," I said.

"Your problem," Cinelli said, "is that your concept of art is limited to naked women with big boobs on calendars in automobile repair shops."

"So?"

Room 6 of the Tate Gallery offered plenty of naked women, I'm pleased to say. It was a celebration of female nudity, from the front, the rear, and all sides. There were praying nudes, evil nudes, farming nudes, reclining nudes, picnicking nudes, happy nudes, sad nudes, frolicking nudes, and bull-taming nudes. Everything but writing nudes. I have been known to write in my underwear, but I guess that doesn't qualify. Later on, some of the artists who had painted the nudes overcame their obsession with naked women and settled down to paint boats and apples. Age does that to you.

But I will say that the Tate had a better seating arrangement for those of us content to sit in the middle of a room and turn as necessary to view the paintings from afar, even though it occasionally required spinning in the opposite direction. The benches were comfortable and plentiful, so that one didn't have to stand glaring at an old lady while waiting for her to get up and free the space she was occupying. Some old ladies can sit for hours, but a good hard glare will sometimes jar the more timid ones off a bench.

I love London. I love the funny way the people talk. I love their pubs. I love the fog. But I don't love their food. Voltaire is said to have remarked that England has forty-two religions and only two sauces. They still eat mutton and something in a potpie. Birds, I think. Small ones with little bones. We had to search to find good restaurants, and then they were usually in hotels and expensive.

"You're too fussy," Cinelli said, eating something gray. We were in an upstairs pub on a dark alley near Charing Cross. Mad cow disease was still in the news, and I was avoiding anything with meat in it. I have enough problems getting by from day to day without coming down with an ailment that will cause me to foam at the mouth and fall down, mooing irrationally.

"You won't moo," Cinelli said, "and the disease is nothing to make fun of. Would you like a taste of the gray stuff?"

"Just exactly what is that?"

"Meat in a kind of mush."

The waitress had recommended it as a local dish, but she said it in her native tongue, British-English, and we couldn't understand it.

"I'll have some of that," Cinelli said bravely.

"Is it good?" I asked.

"You can't judge it by good or bad," Cinelli said. "It's just . . . filling."

She was right to the extent that mad cow disease, which is really bovine spongiform encephalopathy (BSE), was not a laughing matter. But I found the prospect amusing that while the world worried about nuclear or biological warfare, sick cows might be the ultimate weapon. Use infected beef in hamburgers, and there goes the teenage population.

We toured Oxford and Bath and Stonehenge and the Tower of London and Westminster Cathedral and the Houses of Parliament and Windsor Castle and Stratford on Avon and a lot of things I can't remember. I suppose, as a writer, I am expected to report that standing in the small house where William Shakespeare was born was the equivalent of praying at the Wailing Wall, but it wasn't. My favorite place was London's East End, where Jack the Ripper played and Sweeney Todd turned his tonsorial customers into ground beef.

I have covered many murders over the decades that I've been a journalist and am constantly intrigued by the energy and the imagination required to kill another human being, not to mention the dementia involved. I drove Cinelli through San Francisco and

Oakland once, pointing out homes, street corners, and bars where interesting homicides had occurred. She was quiet for much of the tour and appeared a little shaken when I showed her the place where a serial killer had gone up and down a whole block in San Francisco's Tenderloin, killing at random. Unlike Jack the Ripper, he didn't kill just prostitutes, but anyone who happened to cross his path. When the tour was finished, we stopped for dinner at an Italian restaurant in the neighborhood. Cinelli wasn't very hungry. I can't imagine why.

It was foggy in London's East End as we strolled down the gaslit alleyways. If one had a vivid imagination, one could picture old Jack ripping away at the ladies of the night as he had back in 1888. Makes a guy smile and shudder. Not that I condone killing anyone, for God's sake, but there's something satisfying about being afraid and knowing that it's just a, well, fun-fear and you're neither a victim nor about to become one.

"Old Jack was really some kind of nut," I said, as we headed back to our hotel.

"Old Al is really some kind of nut for liking this stuff," Cinelli said.

On to Madrid.

One need only recall the Inquisition to conclude that the Spanish are not gentle people. I say that even though I am one, although Basques do not consider themselves citizens of Spain, and I'm mostly Basque. They call the area they occupy Euskadi and have been striving for decades to cut free of the mother country. Every once in a while they blow something up or do someone in to call attention to their efforts. But ever since the Inquisition's auto-da-fé fizzled out some seven hundred years ago, the Spanish generally have quit burning heretics at the stake, which is something to say in their favor, despite the abruptness of their nature.

We drove into Madrid in a rented car at a time of fiesta, which, as someone pointed out, is almost any time of the year. It was fiesta season in the south of France too when we passed through once. We do not reserve rooms in advance during our driving vacations in Europe, except for the day we land and the day we depart. Sometimes that creates difficulties. In the area around Nice, there was nothing available, cheap or expensive. We drove far into the night until we spotted what appeared to be a hotel. Cinelli went in to check. She was gone for some time and then returned looking as though she had just been groped by an evil spirit.

"What's up?" I said.

"It's a house of prostitution," she said, climbing into the car, not quite believing she had just sought a room in a whorehouse.

I stuck my head out the window. It was a quaint old building, weathered by time, the kind that adorn the French countryside.

"It's a nice-looking place," I said. "Maybe if there's a room they're not using . . ."

"I'm not staying in a whorehouse," she said.

"But it's late and we're tired and—"

"Drive on!"

In Amsterdam, where prostitution is legal, the whorehouses are lined up along the main canal. The women sit in show windows dressed in revealing lingerie. One bored fat lady reclined under a large sign that read, Fuckee Fuckee, but her demeanor didn't seem to stir anyone's passion.

"I wonder if they have a gift shop," I said, studying the place. I had never seen a house of prostitution before. I swear.

I could imagine replicas of designer dildos and black lace panties with open crotches and 48D-cup bras with the name of the whorehouse painted on them. And maybe one of those satiny pillows that used to say Mom but are now inscribed Fuckee Fuckee Welcomes

You to Amsterdam. The L.A. County Coroner's Office has a gift shop. Why not a whorehouse gift shop?

"You set one foot through that red door and it's back to L.A. for me," Cinelli warned. "That half-naked picture of you in your room is bad enough. You don't need any more erotic souvenirs."

"You took that picture!"

"It was for a private joke, not for public display."

We were in Paris. I was leaning over the sink brushing my teeth, stark naked. Cinelli wanted to use the last shot in her camera. She took it of my behind. I have it on my desk in a frame that features teddy bears hugging each other and smiling dolphins frolicking in the ocean.

"No more erotica," she said.

I winked at the fat lady in the window. She just stared.

There were no rooms in Madrid. All the hotels were *completo*, which meant they were full. The city was a madhouse of traffic moving at high speed without regard to lights, signs, or safety. Language books to the contrary, there are no words for *slow* or *stop* in Spanish. Driving from hotel to hotel was an exercise in survival. Getting there was less important than staying alive. After about the fifteenth *completo* I was shouting at the desk clerks, my face red and eyes bulging. They may have feared for their lives, but it was still *completo*. I tend to shout more when we're traveling. It's my way of relaxing on the road.

"We'll just sleep in the car if we have to," Cinelli suggested cheerfully. Life is an adventure for her. I, on the other hand, think of it as a cruise down a placid river. A float.

"I'm not built for car-sleeping," I said. "We'll drive south."

We checked in Toledo, and I don't mean the one in Ohio. This is the historic Toledo with narrow, cobbled streets and rococo buildings. El Greco painted a lot of his tall, skinny figures here. Ornate cathedrals rise grandly over the city, which is why we say Holy Toledo. Europe abounds with cathedrals of all sizes and shapes. I saw as many cathedrals as bars. Holy Toledo was the same as Madrid: *completo*. Aranjuez was *completo* too, and so were a lot of nameless places in between. It was as we passed a billboard that featured a giant black bull high above the road that I was beginning to accept the idea of car-sleeping. Night was falling and nothing lay ahead but dark hills and open plains. But then as we reached the crest of a hill, a miracle! El Motel! And it had a vacancy! Just one! It was indeed a time for exclamation points! Like that!

It was an hour south of anything in a town called Mora or maybe Consuegra, but we had a bed and a toilet and a store where we could buy food to eat in the room, *olé!* It was almost as good as staying in a whorehouse. I dreamed that night that I was in a bullfight. I was the bull.

We mostly ate in Madrid, because that's where the classiest restaurants are. I am emotionally incapable of eating at "stands" or at diners that serve hash unless I am starving. That isn't food. That's chow. I need decor. I need service. I need to be pampered. And I need to dine at a reasonable hour. Once my body has adjusted to local time, my preferred dinner hour is seven, seven-thirty at the latest, eight in certain extreme circumstances. In Madrid, it's like ten or eleven. Having rested up from their siestas, Spaniards come alive when the sun goes down. I think it's a form of lycanthropy. Every night is fiesta time. They hang out, they drink, they laugh, they howl . . . and they eat.

I should have recognized the Latino habit from a night in Mexico once. We left the kids with Float, the hippie baby-sitter, and went to eat at about eight. The restaurant was empty, except for the help. We were overwhelmed with waiters. They brought us bottled water and tortillas and fun little hors d'oeuvres, some of which could burn the tongue right out of your head. One of the waiters tried to teach me how to drink from a bota, which is a small leather bag usually filled with wine. One can either pour the wine into a container from which one may drink, or one may, if one is a real caballero, hold the bota up, point its narrow opening toward one's mouth, and squeeze.

If one's aim is good and the squeeze is right, a thin stream of wine will enter the mouth and one can either savor the excellent vintage or spit out the foul, vinegary concoction. In my case, both my aim and my squeeze were wrong. The stream of wine struck my nose, spattered my cheek, careened off my chin, and ran down the front of the white gaucho shirt I had purchased earlier in the day for this special evening. It was red wine. I suppose I should have been humiliated, not only at my failed effort to direct a stream of liquid from its container to my mouth, a distance of maybe a foot, but also by the irreparable damage I did to my shirt. But I have discovered that if you drink enough of whatever's handy, humiliation is a lot easier to bear. As the observant J. Belcher might have put it, you get bombed and you just don't give a fiddler's fart.

We ate and drank for the next three hours, as the restaurant slowly filled with customers. The combination of eating, drinking, and touring is enough to turn a strong man into a sleepwalker, and at that point neither Cinelli nor I was very strong. We were ready to sleep, if possible, for the next three days. I called for the check, *la cuenta*, but the maître d' wouldn't hear of it. The show was just beginning, he said. The night was just beginning. Life itself was just beginning.

He brought us more red wine, which was exactly what we didn't need, and moved us, shoving others aside like stray dogs, to a table on the edge of a stage. It was midnight and the show was about to begin. The star was a comedian. And the comedy was in Spanish. We dozed upright through most of it, staggered out about 3 A.M., and slept all the next day. It makes me sleepy just thinking of it.

In Madrid, there were no comedians, just mountains of food eaten late. Our first restaurant featured an open kitchen with carcasses of dead cows and pigs hanging from hooks in plain view of the diners. They were in walk-in, all-glass refrigeration units.

"You sit here," Cinelli said, turning her back to the scene. "I don't like to look at the source of my meal."

I shrugged and changed places with her. "It's not as though we're eating people," I said. "Say, did I ever tell you about the cannibal killer of East Oakland? He'd cut off his victims'—"

"Just shut up," she said.

Our plan was to spend three days in Madrid, dump the car, then take a train from Madrid to Paris and then to Vienna. I love trains almost as much as I love martinis and the Playboy Channel. Our travel agent in L.A. arranged the tickets and said to sign them. I did. When we checked in with the railroad company in Madrid, they were aghast. No one spoke English, but it was clear, stupid boy, that we were not supposed to have signed them. The superintendent would have to decide what to do, but he was at lunch. It was about twelve-fifteen in the afternoon. In Spain, lunch is a ritual, possibly even a full ceremony, that takes time. He returned about three, picking his teeth. He too was aghast, but at least he was aghast in English.

"Not good," he said, shaking his head. He glanced at me, then at the ticket. "Not good at all."

"Are you sure the spirit of the Inquisition is dead?" Cinelli whispered. "If he starts flashing a crucifix, I'm outta here."

Other workers called him *jefe.* That means "chief" in Spanish.

151

He made out new tickets. It took hours. The Spanish do not move quickly. Not at all like the Japanese, who are always bustling around and cursing in their native tongue. Finally, the jefe handed me the tickets with a warning never to do again what I had done. He had an Inquisitor's steely look in his eyes. Torquemada considering his options. I can see myself burning at a stake. I am praying loudly, which is unusual, unless I'm in combat or otherwise threatened. I don't like heat, so I am praying for rain. Where is it when you need it?

"I swear, I'll never do it again," I said in the solemn tone of one reciting a requiem for the dead. We paid him several pesetas and backed out, bowing as we emerged onto the Calle del Arenal. It was good to be alive and properly ticketed.

After a visit to the Prado, which in structure looks faintly like an indoor football field dedicated to God, angels, and bloody warriors, we boarded a train to France, new and improved tickets at the ready. The train moved away and the conductor came through. He took one look at our tickets and recoiled in horror. He had the placid face of a Buster Keaton, and expressing horror must have been difficult for him, but he managed.

"*Now* what have you done?" Cinelli said as the man waved the tickets in our faces while speaking loudly and rapidly in Spanish. The way she said "what have *you* done" strongly indicated that if they hauled me away in chains, she would be like the apostle Peter, who, when the Romans dragged Jesus to the cross, denied ever having known him, as the cock crowed three times.

"Al who? Al who? Al who?" she'd say. "Never saw him before in my life. Never saw him before in my life. Never saw him before in my life."

I had no idea what the conductor was saying, except that he repeated the same phrase several times, which would indicate that he was fixed on a single train of thought. I shrugged until my shoulders hurt and wore my addled-American look with the determination of a master spy. I have my mother's tendency toward a myopic expression when threatened. It confuses predators. Then a single English word emerged from the conductor's mouth, like the deep, clear tone of a funeral bell. "Forgery!" he said.

The man pointed to the back of the ticket where, I gathered, it explained the consequences of forging official Eurorail documents. He hollered. I hollered. Cinelli hollered, and a few others in our car hollered until the conductor finally stomped away in exasperation. It was the most traumatic train ride I ever took. We changed trains in a border town called Hendaye, barely making the connecting train that would take us to Paris. I jumped aboard as it started to move. Cinelli leaped on as it gathered speed.

"You'd have left me!" she said, gasping for air.

"You'd have let me burn at the stake," I said.

"Yes," she said, as we slumped in our seats. "I might have."

It was in the fall and a cold wind was blowing over the Seine. We were staying in a hundred-year-old hotel on the Ile Saint-Louis. We walked, we ate, we rode the Metro, we went to museums. The Louvre, the D'Orsay, the Grand Palais, the Rodin, the Picasso, the Museum of Modern Art, and some others I can't remember. There is only one Paris in the world. One City of Light. And the Parisians aren't as miserable as they are often portrayed. Sometimes they smile and answer questions, especially when they're trying to sell you something.

Whenever Cinelli says, "How about India this year?" I say, "How about Paris?" She says, "I'm sick of going to Paris! Let's go someplace else for a change. We'll compromise." Those are the words I long to hear. It means no India again this year. No filthy monkeys. No polluted Ganges. No clinging perilously to the sides of trolleys because they're too jammed to get inside.

We fall in love with Paris anew each time we visit. I wish I could have been part of the Lost Generation, the American expatriates who came to the Left Bank between wars. I wish I could have sat in the Lapin Agile on Montmartre and smoked cigarettes and drunk cheap red wine and talked literature with Hemingway and the gang. I wish I could have stood by a lamppost in the night and the rain, wearing the kind of beaten, desperate, longing expressions that writers wore in those days. Now they are peppy and upbeat and making deals. I was born too late, too late.

We fell so much in love with Paris on this particular trip that we decided to extend our stay. That meant a trip to the train station, the Gare de l'Est. Cinelli was feeling poorly so I went alone, after digesting specific instructions on how to get there and back. I have no sense of direction. I can get lost backing out of the driveway of our home. Cinelli buys local maps and guides us through foreign places. I drive. I am not otherwise needed, except that I also carry the traveler's checks.

I headed for the Gare de l'Est and got lost. Then I found the station and got lost in it. It was an awesome place, full of aisles and signs I didn't understand and people in a hurry and trains backed up to a rear opening and schedules and noise, all of which tend to leave me in a state of utter confusion. But a kindly bilingual Frenchman, an elderly gentleman who probably remembered us Yanks liberating Paris in 1944, came to my rescue. I explained that I wanted to change our time of departure from Paris for three days and he led me to the proper counter. It was almost Madrid all over again.

I told the clerk what I wanted; he looked at the tickets and shook his head. "Not good," he said. I couldn't believe it.

"Not good? What's not good?" I raised my voice. "IT GOD-DAMNED WELL BETTER BE GOOD!"

He seemed to back away, staring, not quite sure what he was facing here.

"It will cost another fifty francs a ticket," he half-whispered.

That was about another $10 U.S.

"Oh," I replied in a more genial tone, "that 'not good.' No problem."

He took the money, made out new tickets as quickly as possible, handed them to me with trembling hands, then disappeared into a back room. I thought I heard him crying.

The French are such an odd species.

The weather changed in Paris from thundery skies to sunny days. The city performs for tourists, bathing us at times in a buttery glow, at other times in the kind of illumination that lights dreams and fairy tales. Its darkness is rich and enduring, its twilights as soft and lingering as a kiss. An early snow dusted the rooftops of Paris the day we boarded a high-speed train to Vienna. A soft layer of white glistened atop Notre-Dame Cathedral, the Louvre, and the ancient buildings along the Champs-Elysées. It was a magical view of the city, reflected each time from a different perspective. We had seen it in sunshine and rain, and now in snow.

"It's beautiful," Cinelli said.

"*You're* beautiful," I said. Then, after a pause, "Well?"

"You're beautiful too, dear."

The snow continued for much of the train ride to Vienna, a distance of 1,623 kilometers through southern Germany and the foothills of the Alps. That's about a thousand miles. No conductor challenged our tickets. We had a semiprivate compartment. They served us very nice food. The scenery was spectacular. And we met someone who knew someone who knew someone we knew who used to live where we used to live. Wow. Talk about your coincidences.

I try to avoid Americans abroad who are from the same old hometown and ask if you ever ran into someone named Art, but this time I couldn't help it. This guy's name was Fred. His ex-girlfriend Greta was with him. I didn't ask why he was traveling with the woman he introduced as his ex-girlfriend because, basically, I didn't care. Greta thought she knew our old friend Art-something who lived in the Berkeley hills when we lived there.

Oh.

How nice.

She was sure it was us, Greta said, because the person Art knew in Berkeley had the first name of Al.

"Hmmm," I said, "let me think. Al. Is that A-l?"

"Yes," she said excitedly.

"Yep," I said, "that's me all right. And it was Art, A-r-t?"

"That's him!" Fred said.

"Nope," I said, "don't know him."

They fell silent in disappointment.

Americans seek their own when abroad. There is a measure of comfort knowing that one's compatriots are nearby if trouble threatens. Usually, you can spot Yanks by his Hawaiian shirt and her tight-fitting shorts on a fat ass, but not always. There is also a mannerism about Americans that makes them identifiable in a mixed crowd. The Japanese are always aggressive, the Germans stern, the English haughty, the French self-assured, and the Americans . . . well . . . addled. Why do we seem so confused? How can a people who built the West not find their way to a hotel around the corner?

Beats me.

Fred considered himself a fine actor and confided that he might take a shot at Hollywood someday. He'd been Stanley Kowalski once in a high school rendition of *A Streetcar Named Desire* and felt he handled the role pretty good. Before we could respond to his self-acclaim, he leaned his head back, assumed a pained and desperate expression, and shouted *"Stellaaaa . . ."* in an anguished cry that startled us both. I half-expected him to rip off his Hawaiian shirt, and there, beneath it, would be the kind of ribbed undershirt Stanley wore while calling for the oppressed Southern woman he lusted after.

"Well," Cinelli said, when his voice had echoed off down the train aisle, "that was something all right."

"Yes," I said, "something very loud."

Fred smiled.

The cabdriver who took us from the train station in Vienna to our hotel was a loud, burly, hairy man who swore in German. You have not lived until you hear a German swear. The French swear in a language that is beautifully melodic, the Italians in a manner that is loud but lyrical, the Chinese in a tone that is mystical . . . but the Germans are harsh, stern, guttural, threatening, and downright dangerous in their cursing. A lot of *ach*s and *ein*s and *schnock*s. The term *asshole*, for instance, muttered routinely in America at a passing car, assumes a frightening new meaning when a German-speaking cabdriver shouts it at a vehicle that he feels has cut him off. I don't remember the word in German, but I do recall that when bellowed by the cabdriver, it gave me a sudden vision of tanks rolling into Poland and the Luftwaffe raining hell down on Stalingrad. He was swearing and blitzkrieging and shaking his fist and conquering Western Europe all the way to the hotel, *Gott in Himmel.*

"The man was insane," Cinelli said as we left, I mean escaped from, the taxi.

"I'd love to know how to say *asshole* in German. *Achinholsch* maybe."

"That would be nice, dear. Maybe you could learn to say it in several languages and become a kind of foulmouthed representative of L.A.'s ethnic diversity."

"Good idea."

What impressed me about Vienna, in addition to the public transit system, was the *Wurstgericht*. I just looooved the *Wurstgericht* for my *Hauptgericht*. That means sausages for the main course. You eat it with large quantities of Gold Fassl *Bier*. Or beer. Of all the food my cardiologist told me to avoid, sausages led the list. But that was in the U.S. Health rules differ when one is traveling abroad. What applies in the States does not apply in Vienna. It's the air, or something. I felt as though I could eat *Wurstgerichte* until I burst and never have to worry about my heart.

"You keep stuffing yourself with those things, you won't die in Oakland, you'll die in Vienna," Cinelli warned.

How bad could that be? I could see myself as the mysterious Harry Lime in *The Third Man*, my face appearing momentarily in the shadows of an alley, and then disappearing just as quickly while a background zither played the "Third Man Theme." If I had to die, doing so in Vienna has a certain tone of sophistication. Just don't mention that I died stuffing sausages into my face, unless you say it in German.

Since we were spending a good deal of money looking at art, it was essential that we go to art museums in Vienna, which we did. To several. I especially remember the Osterreichische Gallery in the Belvedere Palace. It was my first view of *The Kiss* by Gustav Klimt. It is a man and a woman kissing in an erotic embrace emblazoned with gold leaf and glowing blues and reds in shards of color that grab you by the throat and force you to look.

"He isn't even kissing her on the lips," I observed wisely. "It's a kiss on the cheek."

"I'm sorry he isn't groping her, dear. I know you'd prefer that."

"But it still has heat. I like it."

She gave me a third-grade teacher smile and said, "I'm sure Mr. Klimt would be delighted to know that."

We walked in Vienna, though a cold wind blew down its wide boulevards and narrow streets. We also rode high-speed electric trains and a horse-drawn carriage that clippity-clopped over cobblestoned lanes. We bus-toured the snowy Black Forest and climbed deep into an underground cavern where the Nazis had stored munitions in the Second World War. Our last evening was the most memorable, spent in the ornate Imperial Castle on the shores of the Danube listening to the music of Mozart and Strauss played by a full orchestra. It filled the small room and resonated out into the frosty air. There was a magical quality to Strauss's "Blue Danube" played a short distance from the river itself. And even though Austria's history is filled with strife and goose-stepping armies, and the Danube is dark and polluted, one cannot avoid thinking of Vienna as a place of romance and the Danube as a gentle sweep of water and music that lingers on the memory like a half-forgotten dream.

James Barrie wrote that God gave us memory so we might have roses in winter. And music to illuminate those memories long after our travels have ended. The images never fade. They never grow old.

Shortly after we arrived home, our dog Barney died. He was eighteen in human years, and old age had caught up with him. We were never good friends, Barney and I, but there was a mutual respect. Early in his life we had reached a tacit agreement that I wouldn't dig up his bones if he wouldn't piss on my rug. We honored that agreement until his death. But there was otherwise no way to contain his angry spirit of independence. No yard could hold him, no leash contain him. His dashes for freedom on our cross-country trip more than proved that. I admired his soaring spirit, if not his hostile personality.

When he was dying, I petted him and said softly, "Good-bye, old dog."

He looked up and glared.

Tick, tick, tick, tick . . .

I DISCOVERED VERY QUICKLY *in Los Angeles that the dominant industry was showbiz. Every waiter was an actor, and every accountant, psychologist, lawyer, doctor, teacher, journalist, housewife, cop, and hooker was either a screenwriter or an independent producer. It was screenwriting that made me temporarily rich and crazy. Well, sort of rich, but definitely crazy.*

Television was wide open for new talent to destroy in the 1980s, for writers to manipulate with money and warm puffs of praise up the kazoo. But the summer warmth could turn ice-cold if an effort failed. The money could stop and telephone calls go unanswered should a project crash and take with it an executive's fragile ego. Yesterday's writing sweetheart could turn quickly into today's nonperson.

Money was abundant in this era of excess. Scripts would be ordered on the basis of friendship with no intention to ever produce. Because a network guy was afraid of my agent's wrath, I was paid fifty thousand dollars back then for a two-hour pilot about a rock and roll detective that didn't have a chance in hell of ever making it to the screen.

Other scripts would be bought and then dumped, just so another net-

work wouldn't get them in the event that the "property," as they were called, turned out to be valuable. Network executives, many of whom lacked the creative instincts of chimps, were unable to decide on their own what was good and what wasn't. Their formula was to produce that which was "familiar but different," three words that tailored the requirements of the industry for the decade that wrung me dry.

My only salvation was an agent named Leonard Hanzer, an ex-Army major who stood only five feet, six inches tall but had a roar like a bull elephant. Cocksucker *was his favorite term, and it was applied freely to the heads of networks, to producers, and to others he suspected might do damage to his clients. I worked for a producer once whom Hanzer disliked with a deep intensity. The producer wanted a "developed by" credit on a pilot I had written. Hanzer telephoned the man, who was about the agent's size, and in a bellow that rattled windows called him a "little cocksucker."*

Later, the producer, his voice choking, asked me, "Do you think I'm a little cocksucker?"

I wasn't about to look him in the face and say yes, so I said no and bought the little cocksucker a drink.

I stumbled into television through a profile I'd written for the Times *about a masterful, one-eyed detective for the LAPD named John St. John. They called him Jigsaw John, both because of the manner in which he solved cases and because he was an expert in dismemberment murders and didn't mind matching body parts. He was fifty-seven then, held Badge Number One in robbery/homicide, and came across as everyone's dour and grouchy grandpa. That and the fact that he had a conviction rate of about 98 percent and had never fired his gun in anger made him prime fodder for television, whose independent producers searched for ideas in newspapers like bears digging for termites.*

Ironically, I had written of St. John in the first place to profile a real homicide detective compared to the fleet-footed, handsome young men

who were whirling through a series of dumb cop shows on the tube. St.
John, as it turned out, was familiar but different. God had created him
especially for NBC. Two independent producers saw the story, contacted
me, took us to MGM-TV and then to NBC, and I was theirs. I wrote the
pilot in two weeks and it became a series. I was credited as its creator.
Jack Warden brought Jigsaw John alive on the small screen, and I was
under contract to MGM.

I'd never been a big moneymaker. What traveling we'd done had been
accomplished at the expense of the house. It needed a new roof, the wood
siding was rotting away, and the driveway had potholes that were
threatening to swallow us. In addition, my bathtub needed propping up
due to a disintegrating substructure. It was slowly sinking into the open
space between the floor and the ground.

But then things changed. Because of television, I was suddenly pulling
in five to six thousand dollars a week over and above what the Times
was paying me. I flew the family first class to Hawaii. I bought a sports
car. Let the good times roll.

I wrote the pilot for a second show, Bronk, *and it went on the air*
with Jack Palance. A third was called B.A.D. C.A.T.S., *this one for*
Aaron Spelling, who was supposed to make it last forever, but didn't.
Even with Michelle Pfeiffer as one of its leads, it went down after four
dismal episodes. My star began to twinkle and fade.

What was happening to my marriage was far more important than
what was happening to me in television. I drank, I partied, I said to hell
with just about all that I loved, that was me, that was true and real.
Cinelli watched in horror as I set out to destroy myself and us. We sepa-
rated. But something within, that whispered voice of reason that cau-
tions us on the edge of the abyss, kept at me. And before I jumped, before
Cinelli would have no more of me, I pulled back from the edge.

It was as though I was emerging disoriented from a bad dream,
awakening too soon, unsure of what was real and what wasn't. But as

my head cleared, I realized what I had almost lost. During the wild swing, I had not only taken leave of my sanity, I had also taken leave of my wife and my job. A year passed before I was able to get it all together again.

Cinelli took me back, and so did the L.A. Times. *There was damage to my children from the craziness that had possessed their father. Their stability was shattered, their sense of security challenged. I have spent the years since trying to make amends and trying to figure out what happened.*

I continued to write for television for a few years after that, but gave up the frantic pace of episodic programs for movies of the week. Some were produced, but the scripts of others still languish unmade in a stack of dead ideas in a land where ego dies.

As if to end that strange and unsettling period of my life, the best friend I've ever had, the wry and gentle Jerry Belcher, died of pancreatic cancer. When he told me that his days of life were few, I damn near cried. "I'm fucked," he said, in an observation that was typical of him. We talked late into the evening about our years together, and then when it was time for me to leave, he walked me to the door and gazed out at the perfect sunset that had streaked the sky with pastels of beauty and said, "I wish it would rain."

Three months later, on the day of his memorial at a park by the ocean, it did. Just for him. And as I stood there under an umbrella, I realized that with his death, a part of my own history was ending too. I was saying good-bye to the drunken days of newspapering that had characterized our early years together, and good-bye to the craziness of television that Belcher's friendship had helped me survive. A new era was beginning in my marriage too, based on lessons learned the hard way through self-imposed isolation.

"Welcome back," Cinelli said. I held her in my arms and whispered that I loved her. She whispered, "Let's go to China."

11

The China Syndrome

GOING TO CHINA was an idea that had emerged in our conversation years before we actually made the trip. We turned it into reality, I suppose, as a way of distancing ourselves from Los Angeles and from the trauma that had torn through our lives. You couldn't get much farther away from L.A. than China.

We called it Red China during the cold war, and they called us running dogs, I think it was. I learned firsthand how many Chinese there were in the world during the Korean War when they launched a massive attack against our front lines. I remember looking down a hilltop at this huge valley filled end to end with Chinese soldiers and feeling a little like General Custer in that old joke when he looks across the valley and says, "All those fucking Indians!" *All those fucking Chinese!*

We got out of the Korean mess all right, although much was ventured and nothing gained, and thanks to old Dick Nixon our two countries have more or less managed to heal the wounds of our animosities. We've become, if not kissing cousins, at least tolerant in-laws. So once I was convinced that the Chinese wouldn't cut us up and eat us, as a Marine gunnery sergeant once warned, I agreed to let the roof go for another year and journey to China. And as it so often happens when we begin talking about going someplace, suddenly we were there.

Whenever I think of China, I think of our five-day trip down the Yangtze River aboard the *Victoria II*. I think of drifting through gorges embellished with an autumn mist that made them seem like life-sized Chinese watercolors. I think of a trip of beauty and leisure that felt like a journey back through time, past shrines to gods and demons, and villages that have existed for hundreds of years, enduring wars, floods, and famines in their fingertip hold on survival.

I was the one who lobbied for the river trip, because being aboard any kind of boat relaxes me more than anything else I can think of, except maybe sex or a martini. Put all of them together and I can sleep for a week. Our troop ship en route to Korea was caught in a typhoon in the Sea of Japan, and it rocked and rolled like a carnival ride. Below deck, where they stashed us, two-thirds of us were sick and throwing up. I was among the few who didn't suffer from mal de mer, and I wanted to get the hell out of there, so I volunteered for guard duty on deck.

There's an ancient piece of advice in the Marine Corps that admonishes new recruits to "Keep your mouth shut, your bowels open, and don't volunteer for anything." I mean "for nothing." I ignored that by asking to go topside, as we called it, and topside I went. Describing a typhoon is like trying to imagine what the end of the world would be like. Every sense is involved as the storm embraces you in howls and roars, in mountains of waves, and in flashes of distant lightning. Sea smells, a mixture of salt and ozone, and the stinging spray of the ocean complete the weather's total domination of the senses, an experience I haven't had since, and will probably never have again.

Marines stand guard even when there's no necessity to stand guard, which includes being at sea. During times of violent weather we are attached to railings along the bulkheads of the ship by a leather strap that allows us to move back and forth along the deck without being washed overboard and disappearing like mites into the roaring calamity. The experience was summed up for me that night when out of the booming storm came a gunnery sergeant, head lowered, feet apart for balance, bucking into the wind like a frigate, as one with the storm. He stopped to ask if I was okay, then as he left paused to say, "You'll remember this the rest of your life, kid. Everything else is pissing into the wind." And he was right.

All I'm saying is I don't get seasick, but Cinelli does have that tendency. We were aboard the pirate boat at Disneyland once, and even though it didn't go anywhere it was kind of bobbing in water and she began to feel funny.

"You can't be seasick," I said. "We're not moving."

"It's a psychological sick," she said. "It's in the head."

"Then close your eyes and think of England."

It was a line from a play.

"I'll think of Arizona. It's landlocked."

She weathered the Yangtze just fine because it was peaceful. I became so damned friendly and obliging that I even took a class in making Chinese dumplings, which is totally uncharacteristic of me. I don't join in, I don't sing along, and I sure as hell don't give a rat's ass about dumplings.

We docked here and there to see things, which was okay, but because China had been undergoing a drought, the river was low. That required walking on wobbly wooden planks from the boat to shore, with young women along the way making sure we didn't fall into the mudflats or into the Yangtze itself. Then it was up steps to reach buses that would take us to whatever we were going to see. In one case, there were seventy-eight steps, and by the time I reached the top I had to be pushed into the bus like a load of beef.

One trip was to the Gates of Hell, which sounded mildly intriguing, except that it required soaring above the treetops in gondolas, like Peter Pan cruising over London. I'm not big on heights, even though airplanes don't bother me. If they did, this would be a book of blank pages. But gondolas and swaying footbridges over deep chasms come close to paralyzing me. Cinelli talked me onto one of those narrow footbridges in the Canadian Rockies once, a thousand feet over a roaring river. Death waited below. The bridge was just wide enough for one person, and when some nut came whistling along from the opposite direction and tried to squeeze by, I went bonkers. I screamed at him and cursed him so hysterically that he turned and went back and allowed me to cross, whereupon I sweetly apologized. He just stared and backed away.

The gondolas involved a similar terror. The small cars were made for two people and were attached to a cable strung between a series of towers. The cables sagged between towers and rose as they approached them. This caused the cars, which climbed and swayed over the treetops of a garden below (where a different kind of death waited), to climb upward in a precipitous manner, tilting backward.

I said a flat no to riding the gondolas, which, I have learned over many years, means nothing to a wife. It indicates a slight delay in achieving her goal and possibly even an argument and a pout, but eventually the no proves to be written on sand washed away by a tide. Cowardice was the ploy she used to get me into a gondola. Not "You're a yellow-bellied whiner," but "There's nothing to be afraid of. You were so brave in the Marines. This is nothing compared to that."

It wasn't just the gondola. It was getting on. The cars were on one continuous loop and didn't stop at the station. You leaped aboard as one went by, hopefully settling in before it began its upward climb and leaving you hanging by your fingertips at its edge. We boarded okay and Cinelli chattered happily away, pointing out various places in the garden thirty thousand feet below (okay, thirty feet). I said, "Yes," and, "Oh, lovely," and, "What gorgeous colors," but it was all a sham. My eyes were closed the whole way. At the elevated terminal of the tram there was a series of statues with evil faces and artifacts that contributed to the hellish theme. They were painted in lacquered reds and deep blacks, but I was too worried about getting back aboard the cars of death to notice much. We made it to the lower station without the car dumping us out or the cable snapping or the tower toppling over, all of which said to me how far the Chinese had come in the past two thousand years.

Another Yangtze side trip involved a stop at the site where the Three Gorges Dam was being constructed. This is a monumental project, China's most ambitious undertaking since the Great Wall. It will displace almost two million people and wipe out cities, farms, and even some of the canyons. Someone said it can be seen from the moon, but since I've never been to the moon, I can't say. I do know that it will stand 607 feet high and be a mile wide. Twenty-six of the largest turbines ever built will generate the equivalent electrical output of eighteen nuclear power plants.

This is all good stuff, I suppose, because China needs the power. But gone will be the beautiful gorges from which the river takes its name, narrow waterways with steep sides we negotiated on sampans out of the town of Wuchang. They were motorized metal boats that sometimes ground over rocks on the river bottom where its level was measured in inches. Narrow trails wound up the steep sides of the canyon that bordered the gorges, wrapped in a mist that drifts through every memory I have of China.

The trails and the villages near the top and caves occupied hundreds, maybe thousands, of years ago will be under water when the new dam is completed in 2009. But for three hours we were given a close view of what had existed for centuries, and neither of us will forget it.

They let us off the boat in Wuchan, not to be confused with Wuchang. It's an ancient, musty, and smog-shrouded city in eastern China. Cinelli had arranged our three weeks in China, from Beijing to Chongqing to Wuhan to Xi'an to Beijing again, then to Shanghai, with a guide meeting us in each location. Theoretically. No one met us at the dock in Wuhan, as we stood on a street that was surreal in its wild mix of traffic pandemonium. Mopeds, motorcycles, bicycles, motorized rickshaws, buses, red taxis, and pedestrians fought for space on both the street and the sidewalk in a wild game of chicken unknown to the Western world, except maybe in New York. I suspect that each night cleanup crews must go around picking up the dead and hauling them off to mass graves or just tossing them into the Yangtze, which, like most rivers of the world, is polluted anyhow. You try not to think of that when you're floating along all laid back and mellow until someone mentions that the sampans hauling tourists here and there empty their toilets directly into the river.

When our guide didn't show up, we taxied to the Wuhan Asia Hotel, where he later appeared with explanations I didn't understand. I didn't understand most of what was said in China. Unlike Europe, they don't cater to the English-speaking world. The signs are in Chinese sans English subtitles. Even our guides spoke mostly Chinese with occasional Americanisms thrown in. I swear that one of them called me "dude," but Cinelli said he didn't. He said something like *"Hong tuen, duge."*

He was a young man with a jaunty attitude who, one suspects, was late because he was romancing a woman somewhere. He met us in the hotel lobby and showed us to our room, bowed, and said, *"Hong tuen, duge."*

"Did you hear that?" I said, as he hurried away.

"Did I hear what?"

"He said 'Hang ten, dude.' "

"You're nuts. They don't hang ten here. He was probably wishing us a pleasant stay in the native Mandarin tongue."

"They wear New York Yankee hats and Dallas Cowboy T-shirts. Why not 'Hang ten, dude'?" I narrowed my eyes and leaned forward. "Malibu may be sweeping the known world."

"Oh my God."

We would stay one night in Wuhan and then fly to Beijing for a week. Cinelli had plotted out details of our itinerary the way Eisenhower must have plotted out the Normandy invasion. We arose early the next day to achieve that mission. Timing is everything on a trip abroad. Our flight was due to depart at 11 A.M. Five hours later, we still had not boarded the plane. Our delay, we were told, was due to lack of "separation" at the airport in Beijing. It was snowing there, flights were delayed, and of the planes allowed to land, international flights had precedence. So we waited. The airport terminal at Wuhan is long, narrow, and uninteresting. Decorwise, it is postmodern Army barracks, color-toned to dull the mind. There is no bar and only a kind of shadow restaurant. The toilets are stand-up or squat down, depending on the function you need them for. There is no actual *sitting* on a toilet except for one traditional cubicle in each gender room with a door and a sit-down john. There were always lines in front of these, and many of those waiting were Chinese. They didn't like their own squatting toilets, preferring the Western commode instead. I don't blame them. We are as one on toilets, if not on nuclear armament or the annexation of Taiwan.

We finally boarded the plane at six in the afternoon and waited. And waited. And waited. It is at moments like this that one begins to wonder whether flight on a foreign carrier is worth the risk. Every announcement the captain made seemed to differ in tone, perhaps from his lack of efficient English or the fact that no one appeared to know what in the hell was going on. After several hours of sitting on the plane, we were told it would be a "long time" and were ordered off.

"It's already been a damned long time!" a man from Edinburgh shouted in a Scottish brogue right out of a Hollywood dialect school, except that his brogue was real.

"Too long!" I shouted alongside him.

Someone else, a Brit, I think, joined in with, "Bloody right!"

Cinelli shook her head. "All you guys yelling is like the verbal equivalent of a dog pile," she muttered. "Can't you protest quietly and singly?"

She doesn't understand the need of men to bellow together. Women visit the bathroom in clusters. Men bellow in multiples. It has to do with our testosterone. We can't help it.

Several hours later, after waiting once more in the airport, a word appeared on the flight board. It said, "Cancol."

It was close to midnight.

"I would guess," Cinelli said wearily, "that means canceled." Then she added, uncharacteristically, "the assholes." A little testosteronia there too.

Back to the hotel. I judged from the casual manner in which we were greeted by the desk clerk that this sort of thing happened often, where one left for the airport only to return again to the hotel hours later, cursing a canceled flight. Everyone was quite understanding, tsk-tsking and shaking their heads in sympathy as though they actually gave a damn. The hotel itself was somewhere between a Motel 6 and a Marriott, with nice rooms, a decent lobby, and a concierge who always seemed to be somewhere else. There was a gift shop too, but I already had all the candied apples I could eat.

It was when we reentered our hotel room that I discovered my briefcase was lost. It contained our airline tickets to Beijing. No one had a clue where it was. I hunted down, then haunted the concierge, or whatever he's called in Chinese. I made phone calls to the airport to people who were pleasant but only spoke their own language. One of them knew *hello* and said it every time I explained my predicament. I finally sighed after several hellos, said hello, and hung up.

Visions of us trying to board a Chinese plane without a ticket filled my dreams that night. They would arrest us as spies and hold us until I could convince them that American spies would never try such a trick. "American spies have plenty money," I would say. "Buy second tickee." Would I have really said "tickee"? No tickee, no washee? I don't know.

Wuhan, like most of China, was overcrowded. Sidewalks were

shoulder to shoulder and belly to behind. Moving forward was a struggle, but so was standing still. The people stared at us and smiled. They touched us sometimes to determine, I suppose, if we were real or simply holographic images beamed out of Hollywood. We smiled back and touched them in return. Well, actually, Cinelli smiled and I touched them.

"Keep your hands to yourself," she said, when I touched an Asian beauty.

"It's cultural," I explained.

"It's lust," she said.

I expected the single department store in Wuhan to be a dark, cavernous building filled with olive-drab padded jackets, earmuffed winter hats, and cloddish boots for women. *Au contraire.* Think of the finest Paris fashions, elegant leather jackets, silk suits and shoes from the haute couture centers of Europe and America. This was no J. C. Penney's Outlet. More like Saks Fifth Avenue, open and beautiful and expensive. And it was jammed with buyers. Zillions of them. Think of Christmas shopping, Easter specials, Presidents' Day sales, and close-out bargains all on the same day in the same store. *And they were all Chinese!* I quickly tired of crowds, shopping, and touching. Claustrophobia was setting in. We struggled upstream through the masses like salmon among grizzlies and made it back to our hotel. I dreamed that night I was drowning in a bowl of wonton soup.

The next morning I learned that a cabdriver had turned in my briefcase, sparing me the necessity of having to fight my way aboard the plane. Our guide called to tell me about the briefcase, to say the Beijing Airport was open, and to have a nice breakfast. There were two types of breakfasts in the hotel, one for people like me who ate eggs and bacon and taters, and another for the Japanese who ate noodles and sashimi and other tasteless commodities. The kind of food that kept them thin and hostile. I don't know what the Chinese ate for breakfast, because they fed us what they thought Americans wanted and then disappeared.

At the airport, we were once more issued boarding passes and told to line up at Gate 3. The mood was optimistic and continued so as we boarded the Boeing 757. We found our seats, buckled in, and waited. Fifteen minutes later, we were told to get off. The captain announced that it would be a wait of at least three hours, and added, "Who knows?" By now I was convinced we would never leave Wuhan. The Chinese had never forgiven me for shooting at them during the Korean War, though I doubt I had actually hit anyone. Wuhan was their revenge. It was hell.

Four hours passed in the waiting room before we were once more told to go aboard. For three more hours we sat in the plane. They fed us and we waited. Then the captain ordered us off again. That did it. The Japanese refused to leave. They were beyond furious. They yelled and shook their fists and swore in a mixture of Japanese and English, which I am certain incorporated the foulest elements of both languages. Their rage had actually begun in the airport itself, with their ranting against clerks and police and anyone else who was either in uniform or behind a counter. They were Japanese businessmen in double-breasted suits who talked on cell phones and carried genuine leather briefcases, not like my imitation leather one, and handheld computers they kept punching away at.

But their pure, over-the-top rage exploded when we were told to leave the plane. One can imagine the same kind of fury in their battles in the South Pacific during World War II. Their banzai charges were fueled by a similar commitment, only this time they weren't carrying bayonets, for which the flight crew could thank the Lord. They cursed the captains, the flight attendants, and the airport personnel who came aboard to explain and apologize, and who finally left in fear.

I'm not sure if that's what did it, but we finally took off at six-thirty. Two hours later, we were in a snowy Beijing, but our pilot had a small measure of revenge. We had to sit aboard the plane for another two hours because there was no gate available. But at least we'd made it. The Japanese strode off in step, looking triumphant. I almost applauded.

China has been inhabited by humans for three hundred and fifty thousand years, if you believe what archaeologists tell us, and has been an empire since about two thousand years before the Christian Era. For those unfamiliar with the scope of history, that predates even the death of Elvis Presley and the creation of MTV. It's just, to simplify, a long time ago.

You can therefore look upon Beijing as either a part of antiquity or just another overcrowded, underfed metropolis that is large, confusing, and expensive. Our guide was Fatima. She had a law degree but made more money shepherding around those of us who otherwise would have been lost in the wash of humanity, never to return, like Charlie on the MTA. She also found judges biased against women and open to bribes. It wasn't the kind of life she wanted. Her father had been a distinguished attorney and scholar who, under the Red Guard's war on intellectuals, had been forced to sweep streets for a living. The Red Guard was China's equivalent of hormone-powered teenagers run amok. The chaos they produced proved what happens when you empower children to make the rules.

I guess wet weather follows us because we travel in the autumn when school is back in session and the Americans who normally clog other countries are back at work. No one really cares when a newspaper columnist goes on vacation, so I wait out the endless

L.A. summer until September, at which time, if we have any money at all and our credit cards aren't maxed out, we hit the road. Snow followed us to Beijing and laid a gleaming patina over the Great Wall. I stood openmouthed in wonder staring at the grandeur of this mighty four-thousand-mile structure that seemed to disappear into mountains on one side and into the snow clouds on the other. Supposedly one of the few man-made objects visible from space, the fortification was begun about twenty-five hundred years ago, which makes the two-hundred-year-old United States seem like a babbling infant in comparison.

The temperature had dropped to minus-eight and the wall was icy. To walk on it was risky and downright dangerous and could send a foolish adventurer tumbling down the very slopes that once claimed the lives of fierce Manchu warriors. So naturally, Cinelli wanted to walk on it.

"This is madness," I said, struggling for a foothold on a path approaching the wall. "I can't even get there, much less walk on it." Sneakers do not have the same nonskid qualities as other kinds of footwear. I might as well have been wearing slippers.

"This may be our only chance to say we walked on the Great Wall," Cinelli said.

"We can skip the walk and just *say* we did it."

"That would be wrong."

"You sound like Nixon. To hell with wrong."

She pointed to an eight-foot-tall obelisk on a plateau just before the steepest climb. It said in Chinese, translated into English, "No man is a hero until he has climbed the Great Wall."

So up the steep and narrow steps we went, Cinelli and her hero, each step, as the irrepressible Float might have said, slicker than shit. But even heroes have to realize there is a limit to their heroism, so I finally said, "Enough!" and retreated, gasping and frozen, to the heated gift shop, where I bought fans and little red Buddhas and some incense sticks.

"There, now," Cinelli said when she joined me in the warmth of the gift shop. "Don't you feel better now?"

"No," I said.

"That's strange," she replied after a moment. "Neither do I."

We were near the city of Xi'an the next day, staring like dumb-struck children at the 2,200-year-old terra-cotta army discovered in 1974 by a farmer digging a well. I found myself staring a lot in China. Every wonder seemed more wondrous than the one before, but this life-sized army carved out of the earth stood alone. Eight thousand battle-ready soldiers, each with an individual face and body, some with horses, were meticulously created two millennia ago to fight for the glory of the empire in the afterlife.

This was the tomb of Shih Huang Ti of Ch'in, China's first sovereign emperor, who unified the empire, began construction of the Great Wall, and ordered up the twenty-square-mile tomb, with its attendant army, ready to fight. It took seven hundred thousand conscripted workers thirty-six years to build the tomb and fashion the army. Standing at the edge of a dig still in progress, one looks down about ten feet at whole battalions of subterranean troops in battle formation, and at others emerging from the earth like figures from an ancient secret world.

Staring fills a need to absorb and to imprint the way a camera never can. I found myself transfixed by this army meant for eternity. And watching archaeologists at work among the figures, I came to realize I was witnessing a part of history, a wonder of the world, being unearthed right there in front of me. It was like stumbling upon the Dead Sea Scrolls, in a way. Only the guide's necessity to move on tore me away from the archers and charioteers that were pledged to fight to the death for their emperor when time was still young.

Guides never tire of moving on. The drummer they march to beats a tempo that is at least twice the speed of ordinary human movement. One of our guides in France, a small woman who carried a red umbrella, moved on faster than any tour leader I'd ever seen. She'd holler, "Let's go, let's go!" over the din of wherever we were, jerk her red umbrella up and down over her head like Mary Poppins preparing for takeoff, and stride away. Dallying was out of the question. In a castle in Marseille, our moving-on group collided head-on with a cluster of Japanese tourists who were also moving on. Their guide was a woman who shouted in Japanese (I'm sure it was "Let's go, let's go!") and led her charges as though they were storming bunkers on Guadalcanal. The aim was to hurry from Point A to Point B, never mind actually seeing anything along the way.

The Japanese, who seem to be everywhere, plowed right through us in a mixture of humanity that totally disoriented me. I ended up following the wrong tour guide and was on the verge of panic hurrying down a maze of halls until I spotted a red umbrella bobbing up and down in the distance. I was never so relieved in my life, even during the storms of El Niño, to see an umbrella.

"Where in God's name have you been?" Cinelli wanted to know.

"With another woman," I said.

A trip through China's countryside is a ride through a nation in transition. Modern apartments next to traditional Chinese homes. Ramshackle stores side by side with gleaming pagoda-fronted restaurants, their lacquered colors aglow in the autumn haze. Highway workers huddled around fires, staring placidly as our tour bus passed, tendrils of smoke carrying mixtures of odors that hinted at pine and sage. I could awaken here and know, without prior knowledge, that I was in the Orient. This land has an ambience of its own, a light and smell that are found nowhere else. I first sensed it in Korea a long time ago, and it hasn't changed.

After the terra-cotta army it was off to a six-thousand-year-old village, and then it was on to Shanghai. I don't mean to kiss off an excavation that housed people before rain was invented, but there comes a time in foreign travel when a man short-circuits from too much of a good thing. Women don't seem to ever reach that point. You can walk a tourist mile and see a hundred men lying by the wayside, either exhausted or dead, and the women marching on without missing a step. That's why there are so many widows in the world. I was beginning to feel as though I was about to join my brothers on the side of the road, but Shanghai revived me.

Shanghai and Hong Kong, which we also visited, merge for me into one exciting, modern, gleaming, busy, sophisticated city, and some other adjectives I can't think of at the moment. The neon lights, the restaurants, their touch with both the past and the future are reminders that many of the most amazing cities on earth are not necessarily in the Western Hemisphere. Red and gold Chinese characters in blazing neon light up the night, adding mystery and glamour to clubs, palaces, and restaurants that beckon like horny starlets at a wrap party.

Open farmland not too many years ago, Shanghai was a city under construction when we were there and probably still is. From the window of our room in the Hyland Sofitel Hotel, we could see a half-dozen skyscrapers going up, with large cranes towering against the pearl-gray skyline and workers scampering up bamboo scaffolding. Modern buildings rose next to nineteenth-century homes, religious temples stood side by side with jammed open-air malls.

China is a pickpocket's heaven due to the immensity of the

crowds in these malls and on the streets, but I never heard of any-one's pocket getting picked. I suspect it is because punishment is severe if you're caught. In Venice, en route on a boat from the main landing to Saint Mark's Square, it was similarly jammed. We were standing in a space never intended for our numbers when I felt a hand in my rear pocket. I slapped at it and turned instantly to face the guy whose hand it was. He glanced away nervously while I glared, uncertain whether to shout for a policeman, smash him in the face, or just, well, continue glaring. I chose the latter. It was a strange trip. He couldn't go anywhere and had no recourse but to stand in discomfort, gallantly avoiding my stare. For the five minutes it took us to get to Saint Mark's, we continued in the silent lock, and when we landed, he went whistling off while I gave him one last glare.

"You're tough," Cinelli said later when I told her about it.

Our guide in Shanghai, whose name was Won, professed to be a Communist but possessed greedy notions about making big bucks on the stock market that sounded vaguely capitalistic. He also sounded anti-American, which was odd for a guide the majority of whose customers were American. When I mentioned this to him he denied it, but I noticed he sneered at every Chinese teenager, and there were many, attired in American clothing. Won and I could have had major arguments over which form of government was best, ours or theirs, but since Bill Clinton was in office at the time with a presidential erection (not election) that was constantly in the news, I decided against it.

Dining was a treat in both Shanghai and Hong Kong, except when Cinelli decided she wanted some *real* Chinese food in Shang-hai. We walked along the Bund, which was the waterfront, and up side streets until we found a restaurant that looked as though it def-initely served only Chinese food. It was called Huadu Seafood

World. "This is the place," she said, in the same decisive tone that Brigham Young must have used when he selected Utah as the site for the Mormon homeland. She was right.

The restaurant, an upstairs place with the sterility and decor of a hospital ward, was less a restaurant than a gastronomical oddity. If I would not eat live clams in Rome and hairy cassoulet in San Sebastián, I would sure as hell not eat snake soup, spiced goose head, pig's tongue, crocodile stew, chicken claws, or fried eel in Shanghai. I have my standards. Cinelli tried some of the more disgusting foods, while I stuck to soggy chicken. It wasn't called soggy chicken, but it was chicken and it was soggy. But at least it wasn't bullfrog or something called poached hairy peas. One can only imagine what that might be.

Shopping is something else in the free markets of both Shanghai and Hong Kong, especially along the Nanjing Dong Lu in Shanghai, a street lined with enough shops and department stores to stupefy history's most ardent shoppers. As God would have it, our hotel was right at the start of this shopper's paradise, and so, with our credit cards and a pocketful of yuan, we hit the stores. I came away with two jackets, a hat, and still more trinkets, while Cinelli loaded herself down with purses, blouses, earrings, perfume, silk scarves, and shoes. I suppose you could buy them in L.A., but it isn't the same as being able to say, "It's a little thing I picked up in Shanghai," if you know what I mean.

Visits to old enemies in peaceful times prove that wounds can heal. China was a cold war enemy, a monstrous entity rising in the East with questionable intentions. To see its people and view its wonders left us with the feeling that if we can only hold out long enough during times of world strife, the invective we hurl at each other across vast oceans can soften into words of détente.

But wounds to the soul are of a deeper nature. I realized that as we departed from China to spend a few days in Korea. It was a stopover I wasn't sure I wanted to make, an emotional walk over ground we had taken in blood almost fifty years before. Standing on a hill overlooking the Whachon Reservoir, where we had lost half a battalion of Marines killed and wounded, I could no longer hear the bomb blasts and gunfire in my head that had haunted me for so many years. The cries of the anguished were muted, the smell of napalm gone.

What I saw before me that autumn day were canoes floating on the water and fishermen at the shoreline. I saw children on paddleboats and heard their laughter drifting like wind chimes up to me. I saw trees wearing the colors of fall like young women at a costume party, and the grass that had turned golden on the hillside. Once the trees were torn and charred by the weapons of war, and once the hillsides were pitted with bomb and mortar craters. But the land regenerates and the flowers grow again.

"Was it worth it?" Cinelli asked as we looked over the broad valley and the distant mountains that receded into a blue haze. "Was it worth all the pain and the nightmares, Martinez?"

I've thought a great deal about that question. Korea remains divided, but South Korea, at least, is free and prosperous, an example to the world of how an industrious people can rebuild after chaos and move on to a better place in history. Several times I was asked by Koreans, when they discovered I was American, if I had fought in the war. When I said that I had, they said, "Thank you," in many ways. Especially the older ones, who knew what it was like back then, and how it could have been.

For that reason and for the sounds of laughter I heard over yesterday's killing fields, I'm glad I spent those days revisiting a dark and terrible moment of my life. I don't want to go back again, but I don't have to. The war is always there, always that wound to the soul that never heals.

Was it worth all the pain and the nightmares?

When Cinelli asked the question, I thought for a moment I might cry. It isn't like me to break down in tears, and I managed to prevent it then by choking back the names that flashed through my head; names of good friends and new friends that now adorn crosses somewhere. Young men, eighteen or nineteen, who had not yet begun to live, who died in the bitter cold or the blazing sun of a war few now recall.

"Yes," I said to her. "I guess so."

She hugged me and we went home. And when no one was looking and no one was listening, I cried the hard and bitter tears of war's memory.

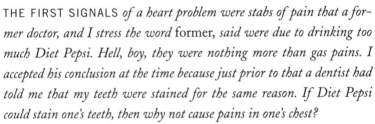

THE FIRST SIGNALS *of a heart problem were stabs of pain that a former doctor, and I stress the word* former, *said were due to drinking too much Diet Pepsi. Hell, boy, they were nothing more than gas pains. I accepted his conclusion at the time because just prior to that a dentist had told me that my teeth were stained for the same reason. If Diet Pepsi could stain one's teeth, then why not cause pains in one's chest?*

The logic was compelling, so I gave up Diet Pepsi and forgot about the pain until it reoccurred, and this time it doubled me over. A wiser doctor, eschewing the Diet Pepsi diagnosis, had me take a treadmill test. He was a young, preppy-looking cardiologist whose father had pioneered in open-heart surgery for infants. I hoped his talents had been passed on to the son.

The treadmill test revealed a problem, and so we went for an angiogram, which, alas, revealed two partially clogged arteries. I remember Dr. Preppy sitting on the edge of my hospital bed after the test. He wore chic round glasses and a Brooks Brothers suit with an expensive striped shirt. His manner was relaxed but concerned, a characteristic I was to see often. I'm sure they teach it at the Harvard Medical School.

He said something like "I'm going to suggest double bypass surgery. I'm not saying that you've got to have it done tomorrow, but I wouldn't wait until Christmas."

It was September. That's often the best part of the year in L.A., warm days with just a hint of autumn. If there's a cold snap, leaves of the buck-eye and liquidambar trees wear the colors of autumn, golds and reds and touches of pastel pinks. By now, Cinelli's garden was the pride of Topanga, half an acre of flowers and plants native to the Santa Monica Mountains. Given the colors of early autumn and a soft chill in the air, I decided that God would surely not allow me to die at such a glorious time, so I said, "Let's do it."

That same afternoon I sat on a hillside near our home that looked out toward the mountains and beyond them to the ocean. Embraced by the beauty of autumn, I came to grips with all kinds of possibilities, includ-ing death, which was the most distasteful of them. I considered death and decided, after considerable thought, that I wasn't afraid of dying. But I was afraid of living as an emotional cripple. I would do what had to be done. The next day I telephoned Dr. Preppy and said, "Cut away."

Fast-forward to a hospital corridor and me being wheeled on a gur-ney, half sedated, while Cinelli walks next to me, holding my hand. I am on my way to surgery, looking upward at the tiled, soundproofed ceiling, those little speckled squares that are often the last view of life for those who never make it out of surgery. I can think of better last views. We are in L.A.'s Good Samaritan Hospital, which everyone calls Good Sam. It's part of the Saint Elsewhere nickname syndrome popularized by televi-sion to make hospitals seem like fun places.

"Wait!" I demand drowsily.

The large black man pushing the gurney brings it to a stop.

"What?" he says.

"I've changed my mind," I say, not quite certain what's going on.

He says, "Sure you have," and continues pushing the gurney toward the operating room.

I mutter only half coherently that I'm going to beat the crap out of him, and Cinelli leans forward, smiling slightly, and whispers, "He's pretty big, dear. Maybe you should wait until later and just write the crap out of him."

I notice there are tears in her eyes.

Time collapses during periods of stress into a few critical moments. I remember little from that point until I awoke hours later tugging at the tube in my nose. It seemed as though only minutes had passed. Cinelli was still by my side, and my daughter Linda was with her. The room was filled with flowers. Dr. Preppy was there with two other cardiologists, one a pert, cute woman with a Peter Pan haircut and the other a handsome French doctor with a disarming accent. For a moment, I thought I was on a soundstage.

My first words were "Are we shooting a movie?"

Cinelli would say later that she knew from the irony in my tone that I would survive okay. I did. I was out of the hospital in six days and writing my column again a couple of weeks later. I returned to a world unchanged from the one I had left. The Jews and Arabs were still bumping bellies in the Middle East. South America was in chaos. Europe was a mess. And in L.A., gang bangers armed with Uzis were refining their assaults on each other by missing each other and killing old people and babies instead.

It's odd when one deals with the possibilities of death and returns to the sweetness of life only to discover how sad and calamitous it can be. When I was able to, I went back to that place on the mountainside where I had first come to grips with the inadequacies of a body growing old. I looked out at the blue-gray distance and I said, "To hell with it."

But that wasn't the end. I don't think the heart likes being tampered with. Some months after the bypass, I was lying on the couch watching Buffy the Vampire Slayer kick ghoulish ass when my heart began to race.

It began with a funny feeling in my chest and escalated to a pounding, like Poe's "Tell-Tale Heart." I wondered briefly if Cinelli had buried someone in the basement and it was their heart beating. But then I realized we didn't have a basement.

I had become expert by then at monitoring my own heartbeat. One almost instinctively acquires that knowledge necessary to remain alive. Gazelles in lion country learn to study water holes before they approach them. Ducks learn not to fly in the paté country of France. I learned to take my pulse.

It had pounded upward from a normal 80 to 120 beats a minute. Since I was lying on the couch, I knew it couldn't be from physical exertion, and I was reasonably certain that it wasn't from the emotional excitement of watching Buffy crotch-kick a high school werewolf. Lying there did nothing to bring it down, so I did what any man would do in such a dire emergency. I called my wife.

Cell phones had come into blossom in L.A. by then, sprouting like shasta daisies in an early spring, and Cinelli had one. I wouldn't call 911, because I didn't want to bother the firemen, who were probably busy playing volleyball or horseshoes or whatever the hell firemen play, and Cinelli was the only other one I could think of. To begin with, even if she weren't available, I could leave a message and she would return the call, a response unknown in the medical profession.

She hurried home and took me to emergency. By then my heart rate had returned to normal, so my explanation to the attending cardiologist was the medical equivalent of a car that never makes a funny noise when the mechanic is listening. I was given a pill to take when my heart rate escalated, but that didn't help. It jumped up a few more times, and during each incident I was taken to emergency, where it had by then returned to normal. I could tell by the look on their faces that they thought I was, for reasons of my own, hearing a funny sound in my car that had never been there in the first place. *The cardiologist gave me different pills and sent me on my way.*

Then one day I was shopping for Levis at Sears when it happened again, big time. *I remember distinctly that I was reaching for a pair of loose-fit 540s to accommodate an expanding waistline when my heart rate leaped upward without any warning at all and I hit the floor with a thud. It happened so fast, I didn't realize for a moment that I was on the floor, and when I did, I wondered why. It occurred to me after a few seconds as I rose to a sitting position, that I had blacked out.*

One is judged in L.A. partly by where one shops, and since it wouldn't be appropriate for a man in my position to be seen dying at Sears, I managed to struggle to my feet. No one had seen me collapse, thank God, and as I stood there I reminded myself to make a note to Cinelli that if I should die at an inappropriate shopping center, my body was to be taken immediately to Saks Fifth Avenue and dumped among the Armani suits. Only then was the coroner to be called.

I didn't die. I found my wife in another part of Sears and she hauled me off to emergency again. They had become so accustomed to seeing me there that when I entered, the check-in nurse said, "The usual?" To cut to the chase, everyone was getting a little tired of me coming in, so they took me upstairs and implanted a pacemaker in my chest to regulate the heartbeat. I felt a little robotic at first, like the machines in R.U.R., but here again, though patched together and wondering how much more patching they can do, I'm still here. Like the old Timex commercials, I can take a licking but keep on ticking. And so why not go to Greece?

Tick, tick, tick, tick . . .

12

Golden Greece

GRANDCHILDREN ADORN OUR LIVES. We have five. This is the year of our fiftieth wedding anniversary and the last year in the seventh decade of our lives. I continue to toil at columns for the *L.A.* by God *Times*, walking the streets, driving the freeways, finding new places and new people in this vast heterogeneous mix of thirteen million souls. Editors and publishers come and go, typefaces change, formats shift, columns move from here to there. I endure, writing the words and singing the songs, prowling like an old alley cat through the lives of those I gather into my paragraphs.

I still drink martinis and have begun a collection of martini glasses of different sizes and colors that gleam on a glass shelf before a window next to my word processor. One is said to have belonged to Loretta Young or maybe Joan Crawford, I can't remember which one, but I think it was the one that beat her kid with a wire coat hanger. Sometimes around midnight I can hear an eerie sipping sound and know it is the ghost of Jerry Belcher having a little something from one of the glasses, still appreciating in his flawed wisdom this prince of all drinks. Martinis always did seem a little spiritual to him.

Glasses, books by the dozens, maps, *stuff*. I look around this small home office of mine on a hill in green Topanga Canyon, at the electronic gadgetry I possess: a computer, a scanner, a fax machine, a copier, three telephone lines, a stereo, and a cable-connected TV set with 220 channels. Once I wrote on an old Remington manual typewriter on a door converted to a desk in a small corner of the house, and that was all I needed. Now all of this, and somehow I can't get along without it.

"Look at it this way," Cinelli said as we discussed the electronic changes that have marked our years together. "Without all this, we'd probably still be in Oakland."

The logic escaped me, but I said, "You know what? You're right."

And we began talking about Greece.

We don't really need an excuse to travel. We tell ourselves that it's best we do it now, while we're able, rather than wait until we are feeble and incapacitated in one way or another, or dead; do it now while our feet still move and our eyes still see. That became an important mantra in the months following implantation of the pacemaker. To me, it was a sure sign of growing old. Well, older.

"You're already beginning to drool a little, Elmer," Cinelli chided me one day when she was lobbying for Greece. It's an inside joke. You can tell when a man is getting old when he begins wearing plaid shorts, drools like a baby, and moves to the San Fernando Valley.

I am guilty of none of the above, although I noticed one morning that I suddenly had hair growing from my ears. I took it as a sure sign either that I was becoming the monkey boy of my youth or that something behind me was catching up. Ear and nose hair are a sure sign of age. I may begin drooling any day now, but I will not, under any circumstances, wear plaid shorts or move to the Valley.

We began planning for Greece because a niece was going to be married on the island of Santorini in the aqua-blue Aegean. That was excuse enough to go to the place where Democracy was born, to the land where Plato and Aristotle struggled to make sense out of abstract logic, where Hippocrates defined medical ethics, among which, one presumes, was the advice of my French cardiologist who, when I asked if I could still have a drink now and then after the bypass, replied enthusiastically, "Of course! Have two!" Three? *Mon dieu, non, non.*

We flew from L.A. to Milan aboard an Alitalia jet, barely making a connecting flight to Athens. We had to dash like charging fullbacks through the airport, scattering Italians right and left and bowling over one or two, but they don't like us anyhow, so what the hell. When we finally reached the gate, gasping for air, I tried to explain to the security guard that I had a pacemaker and was not supposed to go through a security gate. I actually don't know why. I was also told not to use a digital cell phone, but the others aren't worth a damn, so I use it anyhow and hope I don't deregulate the pacemaker.

The trip wasn't too long after the device was installed in my chest. I was careful about what I did because years before, when I was a young reporter at the old *Oakland Trib* (it has always been referred to as the old *Oakland Trib*), I had interviewed a man who was wearing the first pacemaker in history. A few weeks after the story appeared, he died. Pacemakers have come a long way since then, but a man can't be too careful.

The security guard at the gate in Milan spoke no English, and we were in a hell of a hurry, so I showed him a card I carried that identified me as a pacemaker robot. He glanced at it with a serious expression, nodded, and waved me on through. It was only after we had boarded the plane, literally seconds before the door closed, that I began to return my pacemaker card to my wallet and discovered I had shown him a Visa card. The man spoke no English, and it was apparent that he also read no English. Either that or a flash of the Visa card convinced him I was an American of means and he ought to let me on through. So much for airport security in Milano.

It wasn't until we reached Athens that we discovered our luggage had not reached Athens with us. It was the third time an Italian airline had lost our suitcases. I'm beginning to think it is standard procedure in Italy. When I shout, "NO VALIGE!" they shrug, wrinkle their brows, fill out forms, and we despair that we will ever see our traveling clothes again.

The Greeks are less frantic and more organized in their search for lost luggage. While they may or may not understand what we're saying, someone must read the forms we fill out, because the next morning our luggage was waiting in the hotel lobby. No explanation, no apology, nothing. But when one travels a lot, one understands that explanations aren't always required. I had my disposable underwear back, which I was trying for the first time and have since discarded. I need cloth sheltering my genitalia, not paper. That's just me.

Greece is a land that embraces. Sitting in the twilight at an outdoor restaurant in the shadow of the ancient Acropolis, its pillars and towers defying time, I felt a part of the country's history. The twenty-five-hundred-year-old edifice was lighted to a pale, ghostly hue that somehow had the effect of substantiating its power of endurance. Empires and nations have risen and fallen over the long centuries, but this time-worn cluster of towers and temples still stands.

At its feet is the *plaka*, the shopping district of Athens, a collection of tawdry trinket shops, elegant boutiques, and outdoor restaurants that all together create a carnival atmosphere through a maze of crisscrossing streets that change names or disappear completely. There is a surreal quality to the area, a dreamlike contradiction of timelessness and commerce surviving in relative compatibility in the shadow of time's glowing symbol.

Our hotel was in this district and I only had to walk a few feet to be in trinket town. I am not a man who spends big sums but one who lays out a drachma here and a drachma there to add to the clutter of a room loaded with, well, junk. Or souvenirs. Take your pick. We patrolled Athens like advance scouts of a Roman army, seeking out the commercial weak spots, looking for gaps in the Greek prices. Shopping is what Americans abroad do best, but to prove we're not just shop and drop like the others, Cinelli and I go to museums.

The subway is almost as old as the Parthenon, clattering out of the *plaka* to Victoria Station. We were looking for the National Archaeological Museum, which was nowhere in sight on a broad boulevard that was not unlike the Champs-Élysées, but without its charm. A woman who spoke only marginal English sent us in a direction that stretched into miles of walking.

"Are you sure she understood *museum?*" I asked Cinelli. "Maybe she thought we were looking for a mausoleum or a moussaka restaurant or something."

"How should I know? Keep walking."

"I'm exhausted and near death. Another block and I'm a goner."

News Flash: Los Angeles Times *columnist Al Martinez died today in Athens while searching for a museum in the wrong direction. Plans were being made to ship his body to Oakland after a brief stop in Santa Fe, where his widow will visit art galleries.*

We found the museum. It was filled with Mycenaean artifacts from sixteen hundred years before the Christian Era and with reasonably nice places to sit. Comfortable sitting places are important in museums. London's Tate had the best and most comfortable seating areas of the museums and galleries we visited, with cushioned chairs and benches. Some museums provide no sitting places at all, while others offer concrete slabs. The seats at the National Archaeological Gallery were somewhere in between. The Greeks did not carve out an empire by sitting on their asses, and the tradition endures that the benches in their museums not be too comfortable.

We took a taxi back to the hotel with the driver warning us it would be expensive. The total cost, including tip, was the U.S. equivalent of six dollars. You can't ride around the block in L.A. for six dollars. But I shook my head anyhow as I paid. I didn't want him to feel he was too cheap and end up overcharging other Americans. It was the least I could do for my country.

We left Athens the next day headed for a cruise ship, enduring a wild ride through the crowded heart of the city with a taxi driver who had eyes in the back of his head. I know that for a fact because the eyes in the front of his head were always turned toward us as he twisted and jerked and swung and wormed New York–style through the clogged lanes. He talked the whole time, but I was so worried about dying in a tangled mass of steel that I hardly heard him. Anyhow, he was talking mostly to Cinelli. To hell with me.

We arrived at the waterfront in one piece and ended up in a warehouse-sized room more confused than a Paris railroad station.

Huge crowds of people, lines everywhere, no one that spoke English, and no one to tell us where to go. Someone finally came up and pinned a round yellow emblem on us and half pushed us toward a line. I felt like a cow herded up an on-ramp for a ride to the slaughterhouse. I just followed, mooing.

We ended up in Room 112 of the cruise ship *Olympic Countess*. Not exactly the *Good Ship Lollipop*, its name was painted over another name I couldn't quite discern and it had a few miles on it, but it stayed afloat. Our room was a small, inside compartment, not much larger than a cell on San Quentin's death row. It was one of the cheaper rooms, but since about all we were going to do in it was sleep, it was adequate. There was room for my ass and a gallon of gas, as we once sang in the Marines, riding a jeep over the frozen hills.

If you're going to Greece, veteran travelers chorus, you absolutely *must* cruise the Greek islands. They say that after asking, with some surprise, "This is your *first* visit to Greece?" Substitute the word *China* or *Russia* or *Afghanistan* for *Greece* and you have the warble of the tourist bird. I am always tempted to reply, "No, we've been there thirty-seven times before, but in another life." Touring the Greek islands was our intention anyhow, since our niece was going to be wed on one of them. Cinelli had it worked out so that we would spend a few days in Athens, cruise the islands for five days, get off at Santorini, be a part of the wedding, fly to Athens, and then pick up a land cruise of the Peloponnese Peninsula for five days, where ruins of a once mighty civilization abound.

All was working well. We visited Crete, Mykonos, Rhodes, and Patmos and the Turkish city of Ephesus before reaching Santorini, which the Greeks call Thíra. The Aegean was as smooth and pure as a mountain lake. Seasickness was never a problem with Cinelli.

She was too intrigued to be diverted by a physical problem. At each stop, there were ruins to see and mountains to climb to get to the ruins and caves to explore, and gift shops to prowl. I suspect that the primary purpose of these tours is not to expose dumb tourists to the elegant ruins of a past world but to expose the dumb tourists to the stores that line the shores. Due to my addiction to trinkets, I was always the dumb tourist first in line.

"How many flags and key chains you plan on hauling back to the States?" Cinelli wanted to know.

It was something I hadn't thought of.

"Who are they for?"

I hadn't thought of that either. But it didn't matter. Addictions are satisfied by excess. Trinkets were my high. Cinelli's high was climbing up to impossible places to view ruins that were towering structures when Greece ruled the known world. I followed along, as Harry Lehman used to say, pissing and moaning. "Stop your pissing and moaning," he'd bellow, then *whack!* to the side of the head. Cinelli didn't whack me, but probably thought about it.

It was a peaceful cruise until we reached Santorini. Despite advance assurances, no one aboard ship was prepared for our disembarkation. We struggled with our own luggage down narrow aisles, I mean gangways, to an opening on the starboard side where we were to board a smaller vessel for the trip to the island. The ship bobbed at anchor, the small boat bobbed alongside, and we had to almost leap from one to the other, after throwing our bags across the gap that separated them. Then there was barely room enough for all of us going to Santorini. And once there, there was no transportation to the top.

Santorini is a cliff-faced volcanic island that blew its top some thirty-five hundred years ago. When I say cliff-faced, I mean an almost sheer cliff face with a narrow switchback road with no guardrails that ascends several thousand feet from sea level to the plateau on which the city sits. One can get to the top via bus, a perilous cable ride, donkey, or on foot, if you're a Sherpa. Stranded on the shore by the cruise ship, left to fend for ourselves, we grabbed the first tourist bus whose door was open, using suitcases to push our way past a tour leader who objected to our unregistered presence. We weren't part of her tour, but I didn't give a damn. She finally threw up her arms and motioned us to a seat.

The ride up was the most harrowing experience I think I've ever had. Imagine looking down fifty stories from the narrow ledge of a New York skyscraper and you'll have some perspective on our height. Now imagine passing someone on the ledge. Buses manned by drivers who had done this ten thousand times before passed each other like they were on the Hollywood Freeway late for an audition. I didn't want to look down, but I was drawn to the view the way a rat is hypnotized by the swaying of a cobra. I was terrified. Cinelli loved it.

We were trapped on the bus, which stopped occasionally at the top to visit, guess what, gift shops. I kept asking if the tour leader or the driver was going anywhere near the Vedema Hotel, which was our destination, but they ignored us.

"Relax," the tour leader said at one point. "Shop."

"I don't want to goddamn shop!" I shouted. "I want a goddamn taxi!"

"You're getting more and more like the Japanese," Cinelli whispered.

But it worked. Either out of disgust, resignation, or fear, the tour leader found us a taxi and waved us on our way. And we found the Vedema.

Our travail aside, Santorini is that place in your dreams that, like Bali Hai, beckons from an ocean beyond reality. Its buildings are whitewashed every year by city edict and their shutters are a brilliant blue, combining the colors of the Greek flag. I remember the island as a sunset scene that celebrates romance, a long twilight pause between day and night. Liz, our niece, and Eric were married on a veranda with a stunning view of the stucco houses and churches that comprise a hillside of the island. The sun was a blazing red ball behind them, setting the sky afire and turning the bright Aegean into a twilight rainbow. Lights were turning on within the clustered hillside homes, adding a twinkling effect to their already gleaming whiteness.

It was a simple wedding ceremony in a fairy-tale setting. I stood up for Liz, whose beauty added to the glow of the twilight ceremony. Her father, who had died six years earlier, had been the best man at our wedding fifty years before. We were college students and were married by a justice of the peace in a small, drab town across the bay from San Francisco. We may have been one of the two or three couples in its whole history ever to be married in El Cerrito. Our reception, attended by a few relatives and other students, was in a garage. There was no Santorini for us back then. Not even a honeymoon. We took up residence in a small, cockroach-infested apartment in San Francisco's Castro District, now primarily a community of gays and artists, and began the seemingly impossible task of trying to make a marriage work. No one thought for a minute that we could.

But there we were at that magic moment on Santorini, fifty years later, staying in a five-star hotel that matched the perfect beauty of the island itself, observing both a new marriage and one that had baffled the pessimists with its endurance. I watched Cinelli during the ceremony, ebullient in the dimming light of dusk, more beautiful than on the day we were married.

I asked her that night as we sat poolside at the hotel, basking in the honey-warmth of the soft night, If we could start all over, would she marry me again?

She thought for a moment and then said, "Probably not."

Oh.

We are not rich people, proving that if you let everything else go to hell, it is possible to travel the world on an income that is more modest than either of us would prefer. We relied on money we had put aside, on credit cards, and on cash available through the money machines that are now popular throughout the world. Right. The ATMs.

They were especially useful on the four-day bus tour of the Peloponnese, the southern peninsula of Greece that includes Olympia, birthplace of the modern Olympics, where athletes competed in the nude, and Sparta, the home of Helen of Troy, whose seduction by the dashing Paris led to the Trojan War.

"Another woman-caused war," I said, as we poked through the ruins.

"Right," Cinelli said, "like the war caused by Mrs. Hitler and Mrs. Mussolini and Mrs. Tojo."

"There are exceptions," I said.

The language of the ATMs was Greek, which made sense, unless you were one of those tourists who demands service in his or her native tongue. Because I didn't know how to read the foreign instructions, the machines didn't work all the time.

"Why don't you kick it," Cinelli suggested, "the way you kick everything else that doesn't work."

It was too high to kick. I have noticed that despite the amount of walking we do while traveling, I am still unable to lift my leg enough to kick anything higher than, say, a dog or a blind beggar seated on the sidewalk.

I ended up going to banks, which meant standing in line and filling out forms in order to get cash on a credit card. It was easier in Greece than in Africa, where they don't believe in lines or an orderly procession leading to a teller's window. They jam together in large crowds and push until the person pushed to the front is finished and another pushed in his place. I learned the pushing game quickly and thereafter pushed regardless of the necessity to do so. And I somehow always managed to get money at the end of the pushing process.

If one is into ruins, as they say in L.A., the Peloponnese is the place to be. As a result, there are thousands of tourists there at the same time even in the off-season, which is when we were there. Sometimes several tour groups gather at the same ruin at the same time, herds of travelers from different countries, each under the aegis of a leader determined to out-shout the other leaders. Imagine the Tower of Babble and you can imagine the intermingling shouts of tour leaders in English, Japanese, German, French, and Italian.

Tour leaders are required by the Greek government to speak several languages, but not all at the same time. I noticed that occasionally they forget the nationality of the person they're addressing and answer a question with, say, Spanish that is asked in Japanese. Or a question in Greek that is asked in German. And so ad infinitum.

In addition to language confusion, speed is an aggravating element of just about every tour I've been on, no matter where. In Italy, we whizzed through the ruins of Pompeii in about thirty minutes, led by a funny little Italian tour guide trying to set a new record in the tourist dash. This was followed by what he kept referring to as a "very delicious" dinner of cold pasta and cheap red wine in the center of a huge empty auditorium run by a man who was enraged by our very presence.

"I feel betrayed," I said to Cinelli. "Tour guides should be like

201

priests or United States Marines. They should care for us. Guido, or whatever his name is, has emotionally abandoned us."

"We're in Italy," she said. "They're paid to be colorful, not efficient. Eat your chilled tagliatelle and pray that we get back to the hotel alive."

About ruins. I don't mean to be blasé, but if you've seen one fallen pillar, either Doric or Ionic, you've seen them all. When I mentioned this to Cinelli, I thought surely she would strike me, but instead she gave me the kind of look that could wither daisies.

"I can't believe you said that," she said as we stood on a hillside in ancient Delphi, overlooking ruins that were what remained of the Temple of Apollo. "Close your eyes. Let your mind wander. Imagine the sounds and sights. Imagine the life that was here."

I tried that in Pompeii as we paused briefly, very briefly, by what had been a brothel. I closed my eyes and imagined the sighs and moans and the ancient women shouting, "Yes! Yes! Yes!" the way Meg Ryan did it in *When Harry Met Sally*. But when I opened my eyes and viewed the hard concrete "beds" upon which the sexual acts were performed, the visions faded. I could not imagine any kind of eroticism performed on concrete. On sand maybe or on grass or even a loamy kind of soil, but never on concrete.

"Yes," I said in Delphi, lying to placate my wife, "I can see the city, I can hear the people, hallelujah!"

"You're an idiot," she said, leaving me behind to climb a sacred stairway to a theater and stadium at the top of the hill, knowing I wouldn't go. It was the last climb on the tour. After Delphi, we would return to Athens for a night and then fly back to L.A. in a ten-hour journey boxed into the economy-class confines of an airliner. It's the worst part of traveling. Only on those occasions when I am upgraded to business class or even first class do I realize how pathetic and torturous it is to fly economy. There's no legroom, the movies aren't as good, and you have to pay for your own drinks. Jerry Belcher always flew first class, even though he couldn't afford to. He believed that if the plane he was on crashed, all first-class passengers would survive. Those in business class would be maimed but alive, while none of the economy people would make it. It was, he felt, part of God's plan to reward the rich.

As I watched Cinelli climb the sacred stairs at Delphi, I decided that maybe I *was* an idiot sometimes, so I went up after her. We stood together overlooking Apollo's Temple, and I've got to admit that voices did rise up from the ruins, although it might have been hallucinations caused by the male weariness syndrome. I've heard that men have a tendency toward delirious behavior during periods of exhaustion caused by travel.

"Isn't this grand," one of the voices said. It was Cinelli's.

"Cool," I said, emulating every teenager speaking every language in whatever part of the world one is visiting. "Really cool."

As I think about it now, looking at photographs and studying our journals, removed from Greece's immediacy, I can imagine that ancient life. I can see them kneeling at temples and shopping in the marketplaces. I can hear the debates of their philosophers and the judgments of their scholars.

The ruins of old empires reveal the temporal nature of grandeur. We can learn that from a distance in school or by watching periodic television specials. But to actually see and touch the artifacts that ancient peoples left behind, and to walk the pathways they walked, creates a special feeling. I understood in Greece as I listened to the wind away from the chatter of the tour leader that while temples may erode and statues splinter, the spirit of their builders endures. It's that kind of understanding that travel engenders.

Now that I'm a grown-up I want to go back and look at everything again, the way one watches a movie or reads a book twice in order to understand what he's missed. I want to look harder and listen more carefully.

When I suggested it, Cinelli said, "I'm ready when you are."

Always.

I TURNED SEVENTY. *Cinelli threw a party to end all parties, with a bartender, musicians, and even a woman with a bandanna wrapped around her head who read palms and tarot cards. She called herself Mischa. Her name may have actually been Melinda or Esther, but in her psychic mode, she was Mischa. The line of those waiting for her wisdom was almost as long as the line at the bar. One woman whose fortune she told emerged crying. God knows what Mischa might have said.*

I thought about retiring, but there's something compelling both about writing a column and about being a columnist for a newspaper the size and importance of the L.A. Times. *Ego grips you by the throat and screams, "Stay!" An editor used to hate it when I called it the* L.A. by God Times. *He wanted dignity. Then he decided that seeking dignity from a guy from East Oakland was like trying to squeeze honey from a bear. "I don't give a damn what you call it," he said one day. Shortly thereafter, he quit.*

At the Oakland Tribune, *I knew an unfrocked Jesuit who, by diligent research, reached the conclusion that the Virgin Mary had not been a virgin when Jesus was conceived. It was the old wham-bam, thank-you-*

ma'am that got her great with child, according to him. He based this, he said, on her menstrual cycle. I remember being impressed by his research and wrote about it. It was my Christmas column. I can't recall ever having seen our publisher, the former U.S. Senator William Fife Knowland, so red with rage. He almost glowed. Not just his face, but his neck and his hands. Had he taken off his shoes or even stripped naked in his oak-paneled office, I'm sure his entire body would have shone with that same iridescence.

He held up the pages of the column I had submitted. He had shredded them with Xs to indicate not only that the intended column should be killed, but possibly that its writer should also be killed, perhaps tortured first. Not since I had suggested that Richard Nixon might be having an affair with Bebe Rebozo had I seen the senator so furious.

"What's this?" he demanded, blustering.

I realized as I stood before his large, expensive desk that there was no way I could adequately answer the question, so I took a chance and just shrugged. I cursed myself later for having appeared so weak and inconsequential in his presence. I was an ex-Marine, goddamnit, trained to face the enemy head-on, to stick him in the stomach with a bayonet and twist it so that his guts would roll out like an unbroken string of chorizos. Gung ho! Semper fi! Lunge!

"I never," he said, his hands trembling, "ever want you to mention the Holy Mother in your column again! Is that clear?"

Once more, a shrug. As I recall, my head was lowered. God, I hate it when I succumb.

To emphasize the finality of his order, he tore the shreds of my column into smaller shreds and let them fall to the floor. It was a lesson I've never forgotten. To this day, I have never mentioned the Virgin Mary in any column, except for the time an old guy on L.A.'s east side excited his barrio by reporting an image of the Holy Mother on his bathroom window. Even then, it was with great respect.

206

Just about the time I turned seventy, Otis Chandler sold our paper to the Chicago Tribune Media Group. The City of Broad Shoulders met the City of Soft Shoulders. Change was in the wind. Up until then, I was as happy as a whore at the YMCA. I had properly trained my editors in the metro section of the paper to leave me the hell alone. My audience was growing, and I was writing pretty much what I wanted. I knew, therefore, it wouldn't last. My cynicism was richly rewarded. Some months after the Trib people had taken over, the hammer came down. Editors were squashed like avocados. New ones marched in wearing suits and ties.

One day soon after, the new managing editor invited me to lunch. I have a theory that when an executive invites a hireling to lunch, his only purpose is to convey bad news. Executives feel that once fed, an employee is more able to accept with a degree of equanimity the news that he's either fired, demoted, transferred to the Gobi Desert, or targeted for a hit. One city editor told me over a chicken salad that if I didn't do a metro column the way they figured a metro column ought to be done, I'd be out of a job. Another told me over a seafood platter that my column was being moved out of the super-circulation Sunday spot onto a Saturday page that no one reads. A third told me over a bowl of gazpacho that my expense account was too high and I had to trim it down or face the consequences.

When the managing editor invited me to lunch, we dined elegantly at a hotel named after Nixon's dog Checkers. We picked at salads composed of garbanzo beans and arugula lettuce. L.A. loves arugula. I waited expectantly for him to tell me I was a dead man. He would smile, stand, dab elegantly at the corners of his mouth with the linen napkin, and leave for the bathroom. As he left, gunmen would burst in the door, their tommy guns spraying me with bullets, blood spattering the fine white walls of the restaurant.

That didn't happen. He asked questions about the paper. I came across like a babbling fool. I hadn't expected questions. One editor, an effete quasi-intellectual whom I had already figured out, had been trying to decide years before whether or not to move me from the suburbs onto the Metro page. I was ready for him when he asked me what kind of books I read. I replied snappily, "War and Peace, Origin of Species, *and* The Rise and Fall of the Roman Empire." *I made the metro section.*

A few weeks after that tense and memorable luncheon with the new M.E., he called me into his office and said, more or less, I was a terrific writer and they were ending my column in metro. I could either become a roving feature writer in metro, which wasn't a bad deal, or continue my column in the newspaper's features section. That's what happens to terrific writers, one presumes. Well, I chose the features section because, as I said, there's something terribly compelling about a column, which is why so many die at their desks on a final, valiant search for a better adjective.

Meanwhile, a sort of Pax Americana had been laid over what used to be Czechoslovakia and hell was being raised in the Middle East. I was born into a world of chaos and wondered vaguely, Is this where I came in? Should I just declare myself the winner, walk away from it all, buy a pair of plaid shorts, and spend the rest of my life puttering? But what would I putter at? I've never puttered before. I don't even know how. Better keep working. So, like a chicken scratching for seeds, I . . .

Peck, peck, peck, peck . . .

13

Full Circle

YOU TRY TO FIT THINGS in. If you have an hour, you work like hell to get the shopping done. If you have a summer, you work like hell to get the yard looking good. If you have a lifetime, you work like hell to experience everything you can. God knows, we've tried. And we aren't done yet. But thinking about it, we decided that the things left undone ought to be handed off to those who follow. We did what we could for our own kids, and they grew up okay. To the best of my knowledge, they've never held up a liquor store, danced topless, or gotten busted for peddling crack in Butte, Montana. It was, of course, all due to our guidance and to the trips we took them on. Now it was the turn of our grandchildren.

Cinelli and I were standing on our Monet bridge one day, overlooking her vast and radiant garden, when we came to the decision that the best thing we could do for our grandchildren would be to open them up to the world of travel. Then we had to figure out how. The bridge, built by a bearded gnome who lives in our canyon, is a good place to think when the weather's right. It spans a creek that runs through our yard, actually connecting two sets of gardens, and is shaded by giant oak trees. The gnome is a master woodworker and the bridge an elegant extension of his art. It fits into the yard like a baby in a womb.

Travis had just turned fifteen. He was our oldest grandchild. We had four then: Travis, Nicole, Shana, and Jeffrey. The girls were three years younger, and Jeffrey, then the youngest, was four. Since then we've added Joshua, born in 2001, our first in the twenty-first century. That's probably it. Five kids to endow with something beyond money. Travel would be a kind of legacy, seeing the world and defining the similarities of the human race. One species, for better or for worse. We all have noses and eyes and ears. We all laugh. We all cry. We all hope. We all dream. We all shoot each other.

Standing there on the bridge one summer day, with sunlight streaming down through the branches of the trees, Cinelli and I decided that sometime in their teens, we'd offer our grandkids a kind of bar mitzvah gift, or a bat mitzvah in the case of the girls. They could choose a place they'd like to visit within the United States, and we'd take them there, even if we had to sell the dog. At our urging, Travis chose Washington, D.C. We wanted to give him a view of the government that would run his life, and be close to the history that laid a path to freedom's door.

And there were other things too. In what the late Jerry Belcher called our withering years, we come to realize how quickly time stretches out behind us and collapses before us. The horizon is not all that far away, and as a result there is a sense of urgency involved in wanting to teach someone everything we know. The young are the targets. Especially grandchildren. And since every adult generation back to antiquity is appalled by the bad manners of the young, we decided to teach Travis how to function in a social environment, beyond don't spit or fart in the presence of the queen.

So we taught him how to overcome the teenage slump while in polite company and how to hold his fork in a manner that didn't evoke images of workers shoveling coal into a furnace.

"Why do we hold the fork that way?" he asked. "Who said it was right?"

"I don't know," I said. "The British, probably."

"They said we had to hold the fork that way? Why do we have to keep shifting our knife back and forth from hand to hand?"

"That's the American variation of the British fork principle," I said.

I thought I had dealt with all the why questions when my own kids were little. *What're you doing? I'm feeding the dog. Why? Because he's hungry. Why? Because he hasn't eaten. Why? Because I haven't fed him. Why? Because I was hoping he'd starve to death and we could use his hide to recover the couch. (Pause) Oh.*

"*You* don't hold your fork that way," Travis said.

"I'm practicing the French variation of the British principle, modified by American aristocracy."

"Whaaaaat?"

"You're really going to screw the poor kid up before this trip is over," Cinelli said. "The way you used to screw up your own kids."

"Well," I said, "at least they don't eat with their fingers."

We visited our congressman, who pontificated on subjects that interested Travis not at all. Clean water and sewage disposal. Nothing about girls or cars or computers. Then we took him to a session of the U.S. Senate where he could watch our nation's legislators doze and schmooze and wander aimlessly. Our government at work.

"That's all they do?" Travis asked.

"Pretty much," I said. "That and give speeches to raise money for their next election."

"You're poisoning the boy," Cinelli said. "They do more than that. They pass bills that . . . well . . . do good."

"Do good?" I said. "That's what they do?" I turned to Travis. "What they really do is bumble along in committees and try to stay out of jail."

"That too," Cinelli said.

Bill Clinton was president then. We toured his White House, standing in a line they probably never had in the George Bush years. The first Bush, I mean, before Dubya snuck his way in. Clinton was Mr. Charm, especially to the women. It drew huge crowds to his place. As we waited in line, guards viewed me with suspicion and eventually did a quick body search at the security gate. Even though the years have turned my hair gray, I am still viewed as a threat.

"It's your scowl," Cinelli said. "You look like an angry troll."

I smiled sweetly.

"Never mind," she said. "Sweetness just doesn't become you."

Travis wanted to know how come Clinton was always in trouble. He already knew, of course, but teenagers have a way of bugging their elders by asking questions certain to embarrass them. But I am not easily abashed by kids.

212

"He couldn't keep his fly zipped," I said. "That's a good lesson. Every time you unzip your fly, there's an eighty percent potential for trouble."

Travis stared at me, not sure how to reply. Later, Cinelli said, "You really came through with the Clinton lesson, Elmer. I'm sure our grandson will remember it for the rest of his life. That eighty percent figure was a gem."

"Actually," I said, "I think it's higher."

You can tell when a kid is truly awed. They're quiet. Travis simply stood and stared at the memorials to Thomas Jefferson and Abraham Lincoln. We all did. They tower in statues as they towered in life.

"But for them," I said to Travis, "we would all be different."

He didn't ask why. He knew.

We took an elevator to the top of the Washington Monument, haunted the Smithsonian museums, and stood before the walls and statues that memorialized the victims of war. One was the newer monument to the war in Korea, a depiction of armed men on patrol, their expressions set in fear and wariness as they stalk an eternal enemy through an endless night.

"That was the war you were in," Travis said. "We read about it in our history class."

It was history already? Like World War I, the Civil War, the Napoleonic Wars, the Punic Wars? Was it *that* long ago?

"They didn't even call it a war back then," I said. "It was a conflict, a police action. Something, but not a war."

"But people were killed," Travis said. "That's crazy. It was a war."

Euphemisms dilute the intense color of blood over time. Wars aren't so bad when they're conflicts. Riots matter less when they're civil disturbances. The deaths of civilians in battle are only collateral damage to a conflict. Screams are muffled by the words we use.

"Yes," I said. "It was a war."

The murder of six million people isn't easy to explain to a kid. Even having read endless books, and having been to Buchenwald, I still can't comprehend Hitler's ultimate act of savagery, or explain it to someone else. It's something that none of us can truly understand. It's too big, too awesome, too horrible. History will have to supply a larger answer at some future date, beyond living memory.

But little had to be said as we walked in relative silence through the National Holocaust Museum. We viewed replicas of a death camp, pictures of those sent to the "showers," an exhibit of the boxcars in which they were shipped, and in which they often died.

"I can't believe it happened," Travis said, as we moved slowly through the exhibits, one after the other detailing elements of the great human tragedy. I could almost feel the cold winds of Buchenwald again. I could almost see the bleak landscape and imagine the cries of the tortured and the faces of the helpless.

"It's scary," Travis said.

On the day we left Washington, lightning flashed through the sky. Thunder rolled through the clouds. It seemed right.

Shana and Nicole were next. It was August in 2001, an infant year in the twenty-first century. I had doubts along the way that I would ever live to see the twenty-first century. Now I am confident I will see the twenty-second. The girls wanted to go to New York, and we said okay. Three years had passed, and the world had changed and shifted like sand dunes on the Sahara. Angry words fired like bullets across uncertain borders flared into violence in the Middle East.

The war in Bosnia, with the horror of its "ethnic cleansing," suddenly seemed a distant memory. Palestinian suicide bombers were staining the streets of Israel red with blood. Jewish missiles were turning the West Bank into a slaughterhouse. The lands where Jesus walked were a war zone. The very air screamed in pain.

But life goes on in the peripheries of mortal combat and across the distant oceans as though nothing out of the ordinary were occurring on the planet we all occupy. It's a way, I suppose, of dealing with disaster, the notion that it isn't happening to us. The wildebeests move on in relative calm after a lion has picked his meal from the herd. We haven't evolved much beyond that.

So off to New York we went with our beautiful granddaughters, at one moment the epitome of cool sophistication, at another children reduced to girlish giggles over a secret confined to their age, like twins speaking a language no one else understands. It brought back memories of our own girls visiting the Big Apple so long ago, viewing with wonder the concrete cliff sides that shelter the busy asphalt valleys below. It was exciting then, it's exciting now. One can never get too much of New York.

There is no way to compare L.A. to the city that never sleeps. We are out here a sprawling, disconnected set of dreams that no one has ever been able to link. Manhattan is an entity, Los Angeles an idea not yet fulfilled. We have no core, no center, no focus. A few tall buildings have shot up from the gray downtown in the thirty years Cinelli and I have lived here, but they remain a kind of uneasy cluster amid the otherwise drab expanse that surrounds them. New York city is a series of surprises, L.A. an unfinished symphony.

But the age of travel offers relatively quick trips to other vistas, from Sunset Boulevard to Broadway, and one can revel in the changes provided by a few hours of flight. Traveling with S&N, as they called themselves, the trip itself became part of the magic that encompassed the journey. Locked for hours in the tube-shaped confines of an airplane, whether you're flying first class or coach, is usually an experience in boredom beyond belief. There is little one can do, short of stripping naked and running up and down the aisles, that can intrude on the ennui of a long flight. But young people energize every experience, and I found myself thirty thousand feet up actually involved in their excitement. They were Wonderwoman, and I was witness to their transformation.

The shuttle from the airport to the city was a magic carpet ride too, unfolding a new world to girls on the fluttery edge of womanhood. I was called upon to *Look!* as we chugged through traffic headed for Manhattan. I wasn't always sure what I was looking at. They pointed to everything new, until the skyline of the city came slowly into view. Then there was only one view that mattered.

No matter how many times I see those towers reaching upward off the horizon, I'm always impressed. No other place in the world has the triumphant shape that sings of *metropolis,* a word taken from the Greeks that means "mother city." The twin towers of the World Trade Center dominated it all.

By the time we reached the Salisbury Hotel, a small building on West Fifty-seventh Street, across the street from Carnegie Hall, the demand to *Look!* had assumed an almost shrill tone. All pretense of sophistication had vanished like birds in a hurricane. They had their own bedroom in the suite we had rented for a week, their own privacy, and, holy moly, their own TV set. And ultimately they could make their own statement in that private place by scattering clothes, suitcases, papers, and snack food from one end to the other.

I'm not sure why a chaotic room has become the stamp of a teenager's demand for independence, an assertion of self forced to the surface by bubbling glands. Of our two daughters, one represented the shining epitome of cleanliness, the other made it a point to show the world how truly unkempt a room could be. The Clean One, as she shall be known, would awaken at two in the morning and suddenly take to dusting and vacuuming her room to the pristine level of a surgical suite. I'm not saying it's completely normal to clean and vacuum one's room at 2 A.M., but I am saying it shows a certain sensibility to tidiness.

The Messy One, also known as the Smart One, due to her high IQ, found it beneath herself to even remove, say, a half-eaten apple from her room to a garbage container under the sink. It would stay there until time turned it into a small, moldy clump of dust that would eventually disappear. It is always a tug among parents of teenage kids whether to allow them to turn their rooms into garbage dumps and thereby learn lessons of filth when the rats come, or to yell them into obeisance. The problem here is that some teenagers don't mind being surrounded by rats and will share space with them until neighbors smell the garbage and the city condemns the house. Other alternatives are to beat and torture the kids into screaming submission or to simply send them to a camp in the Gobi Desert and allow them to exist on their own until they are twenty-five, at which point they can come home again, provided they can pass a no-filth test.

It was, as I think Yogi Berra or maybe Casey Stengel or possibly Dan Quayle said, "Déjà vu all over again," with Shana and Nicole, as far as a messiness was concerned, emulating, alas, the Messy One. But this was New York and it was their week to be them. I didn't have to teach them the Lesson of the Fork, since both seemed to have evolved beyond Travis, in that category at least. Girls are different from boys when it comes to certain sensitivities. Our son, for instance, never left his underwear in the hall, but the girls seem to leave theirs everywhere. I think it has something to do with procreation, but I'm not sure what.

At any rate, S&N got into the spirit of New York, and the city showed off for them. It glowed in the rain, glistened in the sunlight, and brooded under dark clouds, as though nature were giving the kids a look at a great town under different tones of illumination. At night, because of moisture in the air, the lights twinkled like stars up and down Broadway and Fifth Avenue, making Manhattan more alive than ever. The theater crowds seemed more glamorous than usual, and the men more gentlemanly. When we mentioned that to a native New Yorker, she said it was the Rudy Giuliani influence, demanding a better place for people to live. Just goes to show how the beating of immigrants by cops can keep a populace under control. It's like making believers out of a crowd of heretics by dipping a few of them in boiling oil.

I was just as glad, however, that we could take our two beautiful, flirty teenagers on the streets of the Big Apple without worrying too much about human predators leaping from an alley. I am by nature a cautious man, prone to looking for bad things to happen, and in fact expecting bad things to happen, which causes me to be always on the alert. I was especially on the alert with our granddaughters, due to the feminine swish of their teenage bodies. They can't help it. They're girls.

One never knows exactly what children learn from experience, but the world lights up when seen through their eyes, proving to some extent anyhow that the heart absorbs what the pupils see. Cinelli and I have been to New York a dozen times, but it was all new again as Shana and Nicole, on a tingling Manhattan high, lived the experiences that a touch of life in the big city had opened to them. The Statue of Liberty was somehow grander and Ellis Island somehow more significant as our girls climbed the stairs of the liberty lady, and later as we walked through the rooms where the dreams, and sometimes the nightmares, of immigrants were born.

"They sent some of them back?" Nicole asked, not believing that we would refuse entry to anyone. Didn't the inscription at the base of the Statue of Liberty welcome the world's dispossessed through the golden door? Then how could we turn anyone away?

I wish I could have said we don't do that anymore, thank God, but we do. The golden door isn't open to everyone. It never has been, though we pride ourselves on being the world's melting pot, a nation of immigrants whose voices have joined in singing a song of freedom for more than two hundred years. I answered Nicole the best way I could. But there is no good way.

Each of the seven days we spent in the city was an experience for S&N in the best sense. We rode the subways from one end of Manhattan to the other, crammed into the swaying, clattery confines of a mixed crowd that was probably more representative of New York than anyplace else in town. Shana and Nicole loved it and loved hailing a taxi and loved dining in the Crystal Room of the Tavern on the Green and watching rain fall over the gardens beyond the clear plastic sheeting that protected us from the weather. I danced with the girls, one at a time, to a live band while others watched, somehow understanding our relationship and what we were trying to teach our granddaughters.

After dinner, we rode a horse-drawn carriage through Central Park as the rain lightened to a faint mist that touched our faces with the tenderness of a lover's kiss. Watching the wonder in their eyes reminded me of my firstborn's rite of passage, taking her to see the last performance of the Kingston Trio at the old hungry i in San Francisco, where so many great performers appeared, from Barbra Streisand to Woody Allen. She wore heels for the first time as she said good-bye to the trio, her favorite, and in a way good-bye to childhood.

Nothing was ordinary to Shana and Nicole. Everything glittered.

They saw *Fosse* and *The Music Man,* and waited at the stage doors after the shows to get autographs, and then dined at Sardi's. We also dined at my personal favorite, the Café des Artistes, with its exquisite murals and flowers reminding me of a place in Paris that shines in memory. Shopping included trips to more stores than any man ought to visit in a single day, because the female of our species just doesn't make up its mind that quickly. I bought a tie in less than thirteen minutes at a men's shop. It took Shana three hours to decide on a pair of jeans, and Nicole even longer to decide on a skirt. I could have clothed myself for the rest of my life in three hours.

Macy's was the main shopping area, and while it isn't exactly Bergdorf's, it's big and noisy and crowded, elements that make it appropriate for shopping in New York. Somewhere in the exhausting odyssey of moving from store to store, we stopped at Tiffany's, where we bought nothing, but where the girls got a look at what their futures might be if they married rich. For instance, a $100,000 necklace studded with diamonds and emeralds. Just looking at it caused the kind of drooling usually associated with old age.

"You'd have to marry Donald Trump to get something like that," Cinelli said, somewhat wistfully. "But the marriage would probably only last for a few years, so what the hey. Let the good times roll."

I don't think it's untrue that travel broadens those who seek different vistas. The girls seemed a little older to me and more thoughtful as we rode a stretch limousine from the hotel to the Kennedy Airport. The limo was their final gift on the trip, a ride in style in a city of style. There were giggles at first, but then an introspective silence as the most famous skyline in the world faded behind us.

We left a New York and a world that would never be the same again. I think about that every time I look at a photo Cinelli took from the Ellis Island ferry. It shows the twin towers of the World Trade Center standing boldly in the center of the frame, imprinting graceful images of pride and power on a hazy blue sky. In a matter of a few weeks, they would die in flames and take thousands of lives down with them, collapsing into mountains of steel and concrete and human flesh. The date 9/11 burns into the American psyche.

We went to war after that, and as I close this book, blood has been spilled in Iraq and Afghanistan, in Israel and in the Palestinian West Bank. It isn't over. What will the terrorists do next, now that they have discovered that this seemingly invulnerable Republic is, after all, vulnerable? What will we do next? What awaits the world that has suddenly changed once more in a gathering storm?

We wait. We wonder.

Epilogue

We're getting the roof totally fixed this year. No more leaky patch jobs. There have been big rains in L.A. through the end of winter and the beginning of spring. Topanga Creek is full, and the Santa Monica Mountains are ablaze with wildflowers. Our canyon glistens with greenery illuminated by mists that creep in from the ocean.

Rain usually falls in torrents on the canyon, tapping on the roof like a stranger at the door and then building to a crescendo. Low clouds drop their loads before rising over the mountains toward the San Fernando Valley and turning it into chaos. It was in the midst of the last rainfall that Cinelli, watching the water dripping from our living room ceiling into a half-dozen plastic pans, said, "I've had it!"

I was just entering the room when she said it, and I thought it was something I'd done. I have a T-shirt on which is inscribed "If a man speaks in the forest and no woman is present, is he still wrong?" Guilt clings to the male like drool to a baby.

I said, "Please don't leave me, I'll change, I swear, no more martinis, no more . . . What is it you don't want me to do anymore?"

She said, "Get your wet nose out of my face. I'm talking about that damned leaky roof."

It's a way of telling me to stop groveling, based on the drinking habits of our new dog, Barkley, an English springer spaniel who loves Cinelli dearly. He drinks water by sticking his whole face in the pan. Then he comes to her, his head dripping, and seeks attention by putting his wet nose in her face.

"I love you, dog," she cries, shoving him away, "but get your wet nose out of my face!" And that goes for me too.

We held a family conference and decided that rather than spend big bucks on travel this year, we would spend big bucks on the roof. I would have suggested that we simply buy more pans to put under the increasing number of leaks, but she was in no mood to entertain shabby alternatives.

We have a contractor atop our house at this very moment, measuring to give us an estimate. I can hear him scratching around the way raccoons scratch during the night when they climb on the roof from a point where it dips almost to the ground. They're looking for cats to eat. Free-range feline.

Time marches through this book like a determined tourist. Making improvements on the house we've lived in for thirty years constitutes significant moments on the clock that ticks away our lives. These are pauses between travel when we do the things that have to be done. We fit them in with the passages that shape our time, from the birth of children and grandchildren to alterations on the structures that house us.

When I began writing for television, we doubled the size of our house. A TV movie added a deck. Another movie, a small guest room. Each paycheck contributes to the next trip. But when big expenses are at hand, we stay home. So this year we'll vacation in L.A., and then India.

India?

It happened this way. We were talking about the two grandchildren who have yet to reach trip age: Jeffrey and Joshua. Cinelli said that even if we're not around, we want to leave money for their first travel venture, a glimpse of distant horizons and open roads.

"I don't plan on dying," I said to Cinelli, "until we have personally taken them on their first trip."

"You might be drooling and living in the San Fernando Valley by then," she said. "You think you'll be up to five hours in economy class?"

I barged into her trap like a rhino dropping into a hunter's pit. "Absolutely!" I said, almost pounding my chest. "I could do ten hours in economy if I had to!" Grrrr.

"Good," she said sweetly. "Then a trip to India wouldn't debilitate you now that you're in snapping good health. I'll start planning."

She got me.

"There are cobras and sickness in India," I said weakly, knowing in my heart I was already beaten. We would go to India. "It's so humid in Calcutta that even the buildings sweat."

"Buildings, like dogs, do not sweat," she said.

"It was in *National Geographic*. Would *National Geographic* lie?"

"We'll wear light clothing and check under the bed for snakes every night. And we'll go to Goa. You'll like Goa. It's a lovely resort on the Arabian Sea where pretty girls don't wear tops and you can sit there with a nice martini and watch all those boobs!"

I dropped into a Walter Mitty state. I could see bare breasts, hundreds of them, gleaming in the Indian sunlight.

"I'm too old for too many boobs at once," I said. "I've got to think of my heart."

We both laughed at the idea of a seashore filled with boobs along the shoreline of an ancient land, and me gasping my last breath, drinking my last martini, overcome by the sheer immensity of the mammary field before me.

"We have to go to India," she said.

Well, probably. India is too big to overlook. India will not be denied. Wherever we go, we'll learn and grow as we touch other worlds and speak to other peoples. We'll observe their cultures and perceive their dreams and learn, as we have learned, that their dreams aren't much unlike our own. And we'll have one hell of a good time doing it.

"Okay," I said with the longest sigh of capitulation I could muster. "India next. At least I won't die in Oakland."

Did I mention that we visited Santa Fe too? Mom would have been proud. And stunned.

Tick, tick, tick, tick . . .